Decadence

and Other Essays on the Culture of Ideas

BY REMY DE GOURMONT

Authorized Translation by William Aspenwall Bradley

ANTIPODES PRESS
www.antipodespress.com

Cover painting: *Still Life with a Skull* by Paul Cézanne (c. 1900).

This Antipodes edition is a republication of the work first published by Grant Richards Ltd, London, in 1922.

ISBN 978-0-9966599-9-4

Contents

Introduction i
1. The Disassociation of Ideas 3
2. Glory and the Idea of Immortality...................26
3. Success and the Idea of Beauty 53
4. The Value of Education.............................74
5. Women and Language............................86
6. Stéphane Mallarmé and the Idea of Decadence 101
7. On Style or Writing................................114
8. Subconscious Creation 138
9. The Roots of Idealism 154

Note.—The first, sixth, seventh, and eighth essays are translated from *La Culture des Idées;* the ninth is from the *Promenades Philosophiques;* and the remaining essays are from *Le Chemin de Velours.*

REMY DE GOURMONT
From a hitherto unpublished portrait by Hélène Dufau
in the possession of Miss Barney.

Introduction

When, more than ten years ago, I wrote the first article on Remy de Gourmont which, so far as I know, appeared in America—North America, *bien entendu,* for the author of *La Culture des Idées* and *Le Chemin de Velours* was already well known and admired in such South American literary capitals as Rio de Janeiro, Buenos Aires, and La Plata—it was refused by one editor on the ground that he could not assume the responsibility of presenting a writer of Gourmont's dangerous, subversive, and immoral tendencies to the readers of his conservative and highly respectable journal. Gourmont's revenge—and mine—came a few years later when, at the time of his death, in 1915, the same paper paid him editorial tribute, recognizing the importance of the place he had occupied in the intellectual life of France for a quarter of a century.

What was this place precisely? An attempt has been made to define it by a recent French writer, M. Jules Sageret, who speaks of Gourmont as having represented in our time the *encyclopédiste honnête homme* of the eighteenth century, and this is sufficiently accurate, in spite of the fact that Gourmont was no deist, and that he made a much more extended application of that *esprit critique* which he inherited from Diderot and Voltaire. He himself notes the paradox presented by the latter, who, while combating the principle of authority so violently in one field—that of dogmatic theology—accepted it so absolutely and unquestioningly in another—that of poetic art, as stated once and for all by Boileau. Gourmont recognized no such limits of the critic's function. He was, in fact, a fearless, uncompromising, and universal free-thinker—*libertin*—who, endowed with a restless scientific curiosity, a profound irrespect, and an extraordinarily sharp and supple analytical intelligence, confronted all affirmations, all dogmas, in the fixed intent of liberating the life imprisoned in them. "I dislike prisons of any sort," he declared in the preface to *Le Problème du Style,* and he scouted the claims of those who, having constructed a cell, claimed to cabin the truth.

Even the pursuit of truth seemed, to this convinced sceptic of the race of Montaigne, an idle undertaking, unworthy of any truly philosophic intelligence. "It is as absurd to seek the truth—and to find it—once we have reached the age of reason, as to put our shoes on the hearth Christmas Eve." And he cites "one of the creators of a new science," who said to him, "At the present moment we can establish no theory, but we are in a position to demolish any theory that may be established." He adds, summing up: "We must seek to rest always at this stage; the only fruitful quest is the quest of the non-true." Yet Gourmont himself was carried beyond it in his destructive zeal, when he snatched, somewhat hastily, at the theories of his friend René Quinton, the biologist, to which the fates have not proved altogether kind since they were first stated. For there is usually a positive flaw in the armour of even the most discreet "sower of doubts," and how could Gourmont, who took Pierre Bayle's famous profession as his own device, resist the temptation to avail himself of so formidable an arsenal against the pretentions of the human reason to impose its frail and arbitrary laws upon the universe?

"Reason," he says, writing of Kant's method in *Promenades Philosophiques,* "is only a word—expression of the most convenient ways of comprehending the multiple relations which unite the varied elements of nature. The reason is only a unity of measure, though a necessary unit, and one without which there would be such differences between men's judgments that no society would be possible. But this necessity is not anterior to life; it is posterior to it. What is necessary, what is reasonable, is what is; but any other mode of being, as soon as it was, would be equally necessary and reasonable." Instead of any rationalistic system whatsoever, we need "a flat-footed philosophy, familiar and scientific, always provisional, always at the disposal of the new fact which will necessarily arise, a philosophy which is merely a commentary on life, but on life as a whole. Man separated from the rest of nature is a pure mystery. To understand something of our own constitution, we must plunge ourselves, humbly, into the vital milieu whence religious pride has withdrawn us, in order to raise us to the dignity of jumping-jacks of the ideal."

It was thus that, in his essay on *La Physique de l'Amour*, Gourmont, in order to disassociate the idea of love, which, rationalized, has itself become a sort of religion, with poets for priests, sought to "situate" man's sexual experience in the vast vital milieu of universal sexuality, and such were the aim and method of all his disassociations. In them he reveals himself as perhaps the most potent corrosive intellectual agent of our time, after Nietzsche, to whom he owed a certain élan, and whom he helped to make known in France. All he offers is, in accordance with his own requirement, a simple commentary on life—on life as a whole—when it is not, more simply still, as in his literary criticism, a mere record of his sensations; but this commentary is so shot through with the light of his searching intelligence, and with his sensual irony, that there is little in the ramshackle structure of accepted truth capable of resisting its implications. To taste it to the full, one needs, no doubt, a certain preliminary preparation in disillusion, but, for those who have already had this, no intellectual poison is more subtly stimulating—or more salutary, either.

Where, as in the case of Gourmont, the wealth to draw upon is so great, a book of selections is particularly difficult. A word may be added here as to the plan of the present volume. In the preface to *La Culture des Idées,* which gave him his first reputation, and which remains the cornerstone of his critical achievement, Gourmont refers to the incoherence in its composition, which "no preface can either correct or palliate."

"What good is it for me to pretend, for example," he asks, "that these miscellaneous articles are closely bound together by a common idea? Doubtless some of them hang together fairly well, and seem even to grow one out of the other; but, in its ensemble, the book is merely a collection of articles. When Voltaire wanted to give his opinion on a current topic, he published a pamphlet. We, today, publish an article in a review or a journal. But Voltaire, at the end of the year, did not gather his various pamphlets into a volume. He let them follow their destiny separately. They were collected only in his complete works, where, then, it was possible, grouping them according to their affinities, to avoid that variegated air necessarily assumed by our collections of articles."

What has here been attempted is a first *triage* of a part—the essential part—of Gourmont's work, and its logical rearrangement. At the head of the volume I have placed that article on *La Dissociation des Idées,* which Gourmont himself regarded as having "perhaps a little more importance than the others" in *La Culture des Idées,* since in it he exposes his method; and this I have followed with four articles from *Le Chemin de Velours,* which are there grouped together under the general head of *Nouvelles Dissociations,* and which form its natural suite or sequence. In this way I feel I have been able, not only to offer a book more homogeneous than either of the two from which its contents have been taken, but also, in a measure, to realize for Gourmont a project which, as he explained, the conditions of modern publishing alone prevented him from realizing. So far as I know, this is the first English translation of his essays authorized by Gourmont or his personal representatives.

For the hitherto unpublished portrait of Gourmont which appears as frontispiece to this volume, I am indebted to the very great kindness of Miss Natalie Clifford Barney, of Paris.

W. A. B.

Vence (A.M.), France, 26 March, 1921.

Decadence

and Other Essays on the Culture of Ideas

The Disassociation of Ideas

There are two ways of thinking. One can either accept current ideas and associations of ideas, just as they are, or else undertake, on his own account, new associations or, what is rarer, original disassociations. The intelligence capable of such efforts is, more or less, according to the degree, or according to the abundance and variety of its other gifts, a creative intelligence. It is a question either of inventing new relations between old ideas, old images, or of separating old ideas, old images united by tradition, of considering them one by one, free to work them over and arrange an infinite number of new couples which a fresh operation will disunite once more, and so on till new ties, always fragile and doubtful, are formed.

In the realm of facts and of experience such operations would necessarily be limited by the resistance of matter and the uncompromising character of physical laws. In the purely intellectual domain they are subject to logic; but logic itself being an intellectual fabric, its indulgence is almost unlimited. In truth, the association and the disassociation of ideas (or of images, for the idea is merely a worn-out image) pursue a winding course which it is impossible to determine, and whose general direction, even, it is difficult to follow. There are no ideas so remote, no images so ill-assorted, that an easy habit of association cannot bring them together, at least, momentarily. Victor Hugo, seeing a cable wrapped with rags at the point where it crossed a sharp ridge, saw, at the same time, the knees of tragic actresses padded to break the dramatic falls in the fifth act;[1] and these two things so remote—a rope anchored on a rock, and the knees of an actress—are evoked, as we read, in a parallel which takes our fancy because the knees and the rope are equally "furred,"[2] the first above and the latter below, at the bend; because the elbow made by a cable thus cast bears a certain resemblance to a leg that is bent; because Giliatt's situation is quite tragic; and, finally, because, even while perceiving the logic of these comparisons, we perceive, no less clearly, their delicious absurdity.

Such an association is perforce extremely fugitive, unless the language adopts it and makes of it one of those figures of speech with which it delights to enrich itself. It should occasion no surprise were this bend of a cable to be called its "knee." In any event, the two images remain ever ready to be divorced, divorce being the permanent rule in the world of ideas, which is the world of free love. This fact sometimes scandalizes simple folk. Whoever first dared to say the "mouth" or the "jaw" of a cannon, according to which of those terms is the older, was, without doubt, accused either of preciousness or of coarseness. If it be improper to speak of the "knee" of a rope, it is quite proper to speak of the "elbow" of a pipe or the "paunch" of a bottle. But these examples are presented merely as elementary types of a mechanism which is more familiar to us in practice than in theory. Leaving aside all images still living, we shall concern ourselves exclusively with ideas—that is to say, those tenacious and fugitive shades which flutter about eternally bewildered in men's brains.

There are associations of ideas so durable that they seem everlasting, so closely knit that they resemble those double stars which the naked eye seeks in vain to separate. They are usually

---

1 *Les Travailleurs de la Mer,* 2nd part, 1st Book, VII.
2 Technical term.

called "commonplaces." This expression, relic of an old rhetorical term, *loci communes sermonis,* has, especially since the development of individualism, assumed a slighting sense which it was far from possessing at the start, and even as late as the seventeenth century. The meaning of "commonplace" has also been narrowed, as well as debased, till it has come to be a variant of *cliché,* or hackneyed expression—that which has already been seen or heard; and, for the mass of men, who employ words without precision, commonplace is now one of the synonyms of *cliché*. But *cliché* refers to the words, commonplace to the ideas. *Cliché* defines the form or the letter, commonplace the substance or the sense. To confound them is to confound the thought with the expression of the thought. The cliché is immediately perceptible. The commonplace very often escapes notice if clothed in an original dress. There are not many examples, in any literature, of new ideas expressed in a new form. The most captious mind must commonly content itself with one or other of these pleasures, only too happy when not deprived of both at once, which is not very rarely the case.

The commonplace is both more and less than a hackneyed expression. It is hackneyed, but sometimes unavoidably so. It is hackneyed, but so universally accepted that it comes consequently to be called a truth. Most truths which travel the world (truths are great travellers) may be regarded as commonplaces, that is to say, associations of ideas common to a large number of men, none of whom would dare deliberately to disassociate them. Man, in spite of his lying tendency, has great respect for what he calls the truth. This is because truth is the staff with which he travels through life, because commonplaces are the bread in his wallet, the wine in his gourd. Deprived of the truth contained in commonplaces, men would be without defence, without support, and without nourishment. They have so great a need of truths that they adopt new ones without rejecting the old. Civilized man's brain is a museum of contradictory truths. This does not disturb him, because he is a "successive." He ruminates his truths one after the other. He thinks as he eats. We should vomit with horror if we had presented to us, in a large dish, the various aliments, from meat to fruit, mixed with soup, wine and coffee, destined to form our "successive" repast. Our horror would be as great were we shown the repellent amalgam of contradictory truths which find lodgment in our mind. Some few analytical intelligences have sought vainly to draw up in cold blood the inventory of their contradictions. To each objection offered by reason, sentiment opposes an immediately valid excuse; for, as M. Ribot has pointed out, the sentiments are what is strongest in us, representing the elements of permanence and continuity. It is not less difficult to inventory the contradictions of others, where a single individual is concerned; for here we come up against hypocrisy which has, precisely, as its social rôle, to dissimulate the too strident clash of our variegated convictions. We should then question all men—that is to say, the human entity—or at least groups of men sufficiently numerous for the cynicism of some to compensate the hypocrisy of others.

In the lower animal regions and in the vegetable world, budding is one of the ways in which life is created. Scission is seen to take place equally in the world of ideas; but the result, instead of being a new life, is a new abstraction. All general grammars, or elementary treatises on logic, teach how abstractions are formed. They have neglected to teach how they are not formed—that is, why a given commonplace persists in living on without posterity. It is a somewhat delicate question, but it would suggest interesting remarks for a chapter to be called "Refractory commonplaces, or the impossibility of disassociating certain ideas." It would, perhaps, be useful to examine first how ideas become associated, and to what end. The method of this operation is of the simplest sort. Its principle is analogy. There are very remote analogies; there are others so close that they lie within reach of all.

A great many commonplaces have an historic origin. One day two ideas became united under the influence of events, and this union proved more or less lasting. Having seen with its own eyes the death-struggle of Byzantium, Europe coupled these two ideas, Byzantium-Decadence, which became a commonplace, an incontestable truth for all men who read and write, and thus necessarily for all the rest—for those who cannot verify the truths offered them. From Byzantium, this association of ideas was extended to the whole Roman Empire, which is now, for sage and respectful historians, nothing but a succession of decadences. We read recently in a weighty newspaper: "If the despotic form of government possessed a special virtue, conducive to the creation of good armies, would not the establishment of the empire have inaugurated an era of development in the military power of the Romans? It was, on the contrary, a signal for downfall and destruction." This commonplace, of Christian origin, has been popularized, in modern times, as everyone knows, by Montesquieu and Gibbon. It has been magisterially disassociated by M. Gaston Paris, and is now nothing but nonsense. But, as its genealogy is known—as its birth and its death have been witnessed—it may serve fairly well as an example to explain the nature of a great historic truth.

The secret purpose of the commonplace is, in fact, to express a truth. Isolated ideas represent merely facts or abstractions. To form a truth, two factors are needed—a fact and an abstraction. Such, at least, is the commonest mode of generation. Almost every truth, almost every commonplace, may be resolved into these two elements.

The word "truth" may almost always be employed concurrently with the word "commonplace," and is thus defined, once and for all, as a commonplace which has not yet been disassociated, disassociation being analogous to what, in chemistry, is called analysis. Chemical analysis challenges neither the existence nor the qualities of the substance which it disassociates into diverse elements often disassociable in their turn. It limits itself to liberating these elements and offering them to synthesis which, varying the proportions and adding new elements, will, if it likes, obtain entirely different substances. With the fragments of a truth can be constructed another truth "identically contrary." Such a task would be a mere game, but useful, nevertheless, like all those exercises which limber the intelligence and lead it towards that state of disdainful nobility to which it should aspire.

There are, however, truths that one dreams neither of analyzing nor of denying. Whether furnished us by the secular experience of humanity, or forming part of the axioms of science, they are incontestable. The preacher who proclaimed from the pulpit, before Louis XIV, "Gentlemen, we shall all die!" proffered a truth which the king, though he scowled, did not pretend seriously to dispute. It is, however, one of those truths that have doubtless experienced the greatest difficulty in becoming established, and are not, even now, universally admitted. It was not all at once that the Aryan races connected these two ideas—that of death and that of necessity. Many black tribes still have not reached this point. There is no natural death, no necessary death, for the Negro. The sorcerer is consulted, at each decease, in order to ascertain the author of this secret and magic crime. We ourselves are still somewhat in the same mental state, and every premature death of a prominent man gives immediate rise to rumours of poisoning, of mysterious murder. Everyone remembers the legends started by the death of Gambetta and of Félix Faure. They connect naturally with those that stirred the end of the seventeenth century—with those which, far more than the facts, doubtless rare, darkened the sixteenth century in Italy. Stendhal, in his Roman anecdotes, overworks this poison superstition which must still, in our day, claim more than one judicial victim.

Man associates ideas, not at all in accordance with verifiable exactitude, but with his pleasure and his interest. That is why most truths are merely prejudices. Those that are least open to question are also those that he has always sought to combat cunningly with the ruse of silence. The same inertia is opposed to the work of disassociation seen operating slowly on certain truths.

The state of disassociation reached by moral commonplaces seems to bear a rather close relation to the degree of intellectual civilization. Here, too, it is a question of a sort of struggle, carried on, not by individuals, but by peoples formed into nations, against palpable facts which, while augmenting the intensity of the individual life, diminish, for that very reason, as experience proves, the intensity of collective life and energy. There is no doubt that a man can derive from immorality itself—from his refusal to subscribe to the prejudices inscribed in a decalogue—a great personal benefit; but a collectivity of individuals too strong, too mutually independent, makes but a mediocre people. We have, in such cases, the spectacle of the social instinct entering the lists against the individual instinct, and of societies professing, as such, a morality that each of its intelligent members, followed by a very large part of the herd, deems vain, outworn or tyrannical.

A rather curious illustration of these principles will be found by examining the present state of sexual morality. This morality, peculiar to Christian peoples, is based upon the exceedingly close association of two ideas—that of carnal pleasure and that of generation. Any man or people that has not disassociated these two ideas, has not mentally liberated the elements of this truth, namely, that outside of the properly generative act, accomplished under the protection of the laws, whether religious or civil—the second being mere parodies of the first, in our essentially Christian civilizations—sexual acts are sins, errors, faults, weaknesses. Whoever consciously adopts this rule, sanctioned by the codes, belongs evidently to a still rudimentary civilization. The highest civilization being that in which the individual is freest, the most exempt from obligations, this proposition would be open to question only if taken as a provocation to libertinism, or as a depreciation of asceticism. It does not matter here whether it be moral or immoral. It ought, if exact, to be seen, at the first glance, in the facts. Nothing is easier. A statistical table of European natality will convince the stubbornest that there is a very close bond—a bond of cause and effect—between a people's intellectuality and its fecundity. The same is true for individuals as for social groups. It is as a result of intellectual weakness that working-men allow their homes to be flooded with offspring. The slums are full of unfortunate individuals who, having begotten a dozen children, are surprised to find life harsh. These poor creatures, who lack even the excuse of religious beliefs, have not yet learned to disassociate the idea of carnal pleasure and that of generation. In their case, the first determines the second, and their acts respond to a childish, almost animal cerebral process. The man who has reached a really human stage in the scale of intelligence, limits his offspring at will. It is one of his privileges, but it is among those that he attains only to die of them.

Fortunate for the individual whom it sets free, this particular disassociation is, in fact, far less fortunate for a people. However, it will favour the further development of civilization, by maintaining upon the earth, the spaces required for human evolution.

It was not till fairly late that the Greeks succeeded in separating the idea of woman and that of generation; but they had already disassociated, at a very early date, the idea of generation and that of carnal pleasure. When they ceased to consider woman solely as an instrument of generation, the reign of the courtesans began. The Greeks seem, moreover, always to have had an extremely vague sexual morality, though this did not prevent them from cutting a certain figure in history.

Christianity could not, without forswearing its own principles, encourage the disassociation of the idea of carnal pleasure and that of generation; but it successfully promoted, on the other hand, the disassociation of the idea of love and that of carnal pleasure, and this was one of the great conquests of humanity. The Egyptians were so far incapable of understanding such a disassociation, that the love of a brother and sister would have seemed nothing to them if it had not led to sexual intercourse. The lower classes of great cities are often enough quite Egyptian in this regard. The different sorts of incest which occasionally come to our notice, testify to the fact than an analogous state of mind is not absolutely incompatible with a certain intellectual culture. The peculiarly Christian form of chaste love, freed from all idea of physical pleasure, is divine love, such as it is seen flowering in the mystical exaltation of the contemplatives. This is the really pure love, since it corresponds to nothing that can be defined. It is the intelligence adoring itself in its own infinite self-made image. Whatever sensual element may be involved has its source in the very constitution of the human body, and in the law governing the interdependence of the organs. No account should, therefore, be taken of it in a non-physiological study. What has been clumsily called Platonic love is thus a Christian creation. It is in the last analysis a passionate friendship, as vital and jealous as physical love, but freed from the idea of carnal pleasure, just as the latter had already been freed from the idea of generation. This ideal state of the human affections is the first stage on the road to asceticism, and asceticism might be defined as the state of mind in which all ideas are disassociated.

With the waning of the Christian influence, the first stage of asceticism has become a less and less frequent halting-place, and asceticism itself, grown equally rare, is often reached by another route. In our day the idea of love has once more been closely connected with the idea of physical pleasure, and moralists are busy refashioning its primitive association with the idea of generation. It is a rather curious retrogression.

An historical psychology of humanity could be attempted by determining the precise degree of disassociation attained, in the course of the centuries, by a certain number of those truths which the orthodox agree to call primordial. This method ought even to form the base, and this determination the very aim, of history. Since everything in man comes back to the intelligence, everything in history ought to come back to psychology. It would be some excuse for the facts, were they found to admit of an explanation neither diplomatic nor strategic. What was the association of ideas, or the truth not yet disassociated, which favoured the accomplishment of the mission which Jeanne d'Arc believed to have been received from heaven? To answer this question, it would be necessary to discover certain ideas capable of uniting equally in French brains and in English, or a truth at that time indisputably admitted by all Christendom. Jeanne d'Arc was regarded, at once by her friends and by her enemies, as possessing a supernatural power. For the English, she was a very potent sorceress. Opinion is unanimous on this point, and there is abundant evidence. But for her partisans? For them she was doubtless a sorceress also, or rather, a magician. Magic is not necessarily diabolical. Supernatural beings, that were neither angels nor demons, but Powers which man's intelligence could bring under its dominion, were afloat in the imagination. The magician was the good sorcerer. Were this not so, would a man as wise and as saintly as Albertus Magnus have been taxed with magic? The soldier who followed Jeanne d'Arc, and the soldier who fought her, sorceress or magician, formed of her, quite probably, an idea identical in its dreadful absurdity. But if the English shouted the name of sorceress, the French withheld the name of "magician," doubtless for the same reason which so long protected the usurper Ta-Kiang through the marvellous adventures narrated by Judith Gautier in her admirable *Dragon Impérial*.

What idea, at any given moment, did each class of society form of the soldier? Would not the answer to this question contain a whole course in history? Coming down to our own time, it might be asked at what moment the idea of honour and the military idea became united in the common mind. Is the union a survival of the aristocratic conception of the army? Was the association formed as a result of the events of thirty years ago, when the people decided to exalt the soldier for its own encouragement? This idea of honour should be clearly understood. It contains several other ideas—ideas of bravery, of disinterestedness, of discipline, of sacrifice, of heroism, of probity, of loyalty, of frankness, of good humour, of openness, of simplicity, etc. The word itself would, in fine, be found to sum up the qualities of which the French race believes itself to be the expression. To determine its origin would be, then, to determine automatically the period when the Frenchman began to believe himself a compendium of all the manly virtues. The military man has remained in France, in spite of recent objections, the very type of the man of honour. The two ideas are united very energetically. They form a truth which is scarcely disputed today, except by individuals of slight authority or of doubtful sincerity. Its disassociation is, therefore, very little advanced as regards the nation as a whole. It was, however, for a moment at least, completely effected in certain minds. This involved, from the strictly intellectual point of view, a considerable effort of abstraction which we cannot but admire when we regard dispassionately the cerebral machine in its functioning. Doubtless the result achieved was not the product of normal reasoning. The disassociation was accomplished in a fit of fever. It was unconscious, and it was momentary; but it *was,* and that is the important point for the observer. The idea of honour, with all it implies, became separated from the military idea, which, in this instance, is the factual idea, the female idea, ready to receive all the modifiers, and it was perceived that, if there was a certain logical relation between them, this relation was not necessary. There is the decisive point. A truth is dead when it has been shown that the relations between the elements are habitual, and not necessary; and, as the death of a truth is a great benefit for mankind, this disassociation would have been very important if it had been definitive, if it had remained stable. Unfortunately, after the effort to attain the pure idea, the old mental habits resumed their sway. The former modifying element was instantly replaced by an element by no means new, less logical than the other, and even less necessary. The operation seemed to have miscarried. Association of ideas occurred again in the very same form as before, though one of the elements had now been turned inside out, like an old glove. For honour had been substituted dishonour, with all the adventitious ideas belonging to the old element transformed into cowardice, deceitfulness, lack of discipline, falseness, duplicity, wickedness, etc. This new association of ideas may have a destructive value, but it offers no intellectual interest.

The moral of this anecdote is that the ideas which seem to us the clearest, the most evident,—the most palpable, as it were—are, even so, not strong enough to impose themselves in all their nakedness upon the average mind. In order to assimilate the idea of the army, a contemporary brain must swathe it with elements which have only a chance or current relation with the main idea. A humble politician cannot, doubtless, be expected to adopt Napoleon's simple idea of an army as a sword. Very simple ideas lie within the reach of very complicated minds only. It seems, however, that it should not be absurd to regard the army merely as the exteriorized force of a nation, and then to demand of this particular force only those very qualities which are demanded of force in general. But perhaps even this is too simple?

What excellent opportunities the present offers for one who would study the mechanism of the association and disassociation of ideas! We often talk of ideas. We write on the evolution of ideas. Yet no word is vaguer or more ill-defined. There are naïve writers who hold forth on the Idea, with a capital I. There are co-operative societies that start out suddenly in quest of the Idea. There are people who devote themselves to the Idea, who live with their gaze fixed upon the Idea. Just what is meant by such rambling? That is what I have never been able to understand. Employed thus, alone, the word is perhaps a corruption of the word Ideal. Is the modifying term perhaps understood also? Is it a stray fragment of the Hegelian philosophy which the slow advance of the great social glacier has, in passing, deposited in certain heads, where it rolls and clatters about like a rock? No one knows. Employed as a relative, the word is not much clearer in ordinary phraseologies. Its primitive meaning is too far forgotten, as well as the fact that an idea is nothing but an image that has reached the state of abstraction, of notion; but it is forgotten also that, in order to be entitled to the name of idea, a notion must be free from all compromise with the contingent. A notion, reaching the estate of idea, has become indisputable. It is a cipher, a sign—one of the letters in the alphabet of thought.

Ideas cannot be classed as true and false. The idea is necessarily true. An idea that can be disputed is an idea mingled with concrete notions, that is to say, a truth. The work of disassociation tends, precisely, to free the truth from all its fragile part, in order to obtain the pure, one, and consequently unassailable idea. But if words were never used save in their unique and absolute sense, connected discourse would be difficult. There must be left a little of that vagueness and flexibility which usage has given them; and, in particular, too much stress must not be laid upon the gap separating the abstract from the concrete. There is an intermediate state between ice and water—that in which the latter begins to congeal, when it still cracks and yields under the pressure of the hand plunged into it. Perhaps we should not even demand that the words contained in philosophic handbooks should abdicate all pretension to ambiguity.

The idea of army, which aroused serious polemics, and which was liberated an instant, only to be obscured anew, is one of those that border on the concrete and cannot be spoken of without minute references to reality. The idea of justice, on the contrary, can be considered in itself, *in abstracto*. In the inquiry made by M. Ribot on the subject of general ideas, almost all those who heard the word Justice pronounced, saw, in their mind's eye, the legendary lady with the scales. There is, in this traditional representation of an abstract idea, a notion of the very origin of that idea.

The idea of justice is, in fact, nothing but the idea of equilibrium. Justice is the dead-point in a series of acts—the ideal point at which contrary forces neutralize each other to produce inertia. Life which had passed this dead-point of absolute justice could not longer live, since the idea of life, identical with that of a conflict of forces, is necessarily the idea of justice. The reign of justice could only be the reign of silence and of petrification. Mouths cease to speak—vain organs of stupefied brains—and arms uplifted in suspended gesture describe nothing further in the frozen air. Theologians situated justice beyond the world, in eternity. There only can it be conceived, and there only can it, without danger to life, exercise once and for all its tyranny which knows but one sort of decree, the decree of death. The idea of justice, then, clearly belongs to the series of ideas that are indisputable and undemonstrable. Nothing can be done with it in its pure state. It must be associated with some element of fact, or we must cease using a word which corresponds only to an inconceivable entity. To tell the truth, the idea of justice is perhaps here disassociated for the first time. Under this name men allege sometimes the idea of punishment, which is very familiar to them, sometimes the idea of non-punishment—a neutral idea, mere shadow of the former. It is question of punishing the guilty and of not disturbing the innocent—a distinction which, in order to be comprehensible, would immediately imply a definition of guilt and a definition of innocence. That is difficult, these words from the moral dictionary having today nothing but a dwindling and entirely relative significance. And why, it might be asked, should a guilty man be punished? It would seem, on the contrary, as if the innocent man, who is supposed to be healthy and normal, were much more capable of supporting punishment than the guilty man, who is sick and weakly. Why should not the imbecile, who has let himself be robbed, be punished instead of the robber, who has certain excuses to offer? That is what justice would decree if, instead of a theological conception, it were still, as at Sparta, an imitation of nature. Nothing exists save by virtue of disequilibrium, of injustice. Every existence is a theft practised upon other existences. No life flourishes except in a cemetery. If, instead of being the denier of natural laws, humanity wished to become their auxiliary, it would seek to protect the strong against the coalition of the weak, and give the people to the aristocrats as a footstool. It would seem, on the contrary, as if that which is today understood by justice were, simultaneously with the punishment of the guilty, the extermination of the strong, and, simultaneously with the non-punishment of the innocent, the exaltation of the humble. The origin of this complex, bastard, hypocritical idea should then be sought in the Gospel, in the "woe to the rich" of the Jewish demagogues. Thus understood, the idea of justice appears contaminated at once by hatred and by envy. It no longer retains anything of its original meaning, and one cannot attempt its analysis without danger of being duped by the vulgar meaning of the words. Yet, with a little care, it would be seen that the depreciation of this useful term arose originally from a confusion between the idea of right and the idea of punishment. The day when justice came to mean sometimes criminal justice, sometimes civil justice, the world confused these two practical notions, and the teachers of the people, incapable of a serious effort of disassociation, have come to magnify a misunderstanding which, moreover, serves their own interests. The real idea of justice appears then, finally, as quite non-existent in the very word which figures in the human vocabulary. This word resolves itself, on analysis, into elements which are still very complex, and among which may be distinguished the idea of right and the idea of punishment. But there is so much that is illogical in this curious coupling, that we should be inclined to doubt the accuracy of our operation, did not the social facts furnish its proof.

We might here examine this question: do abstract words really exist for the people, for the average man? Probably not. It would even seem as if the same word attained only graduated stages of abstraction, according to the degree of intellectual culture. The pure idea is more or less contaminated by concern for personal, caste or group interests, and the word justice, for example, thus clothes all sorts of particular and limited meanings under the weight of which its supreme sense disappears, overwhelmed.

The moment an idea is disassociated and it enters thus, quite naked, into circulation, it begins to pick up, in the course of its wanderings, all sorts of parasitic vegetations. Sometimes the original organism disappears entirely, devoured by the egoistic colonies which develop in it. A very amusing example of the way in which ideas are thus deflected was recently given by the corporation of house-painters, at the ceremony called the "Triumph of the Republic." These workmen carried a banner on which their demands for social justice were summed up in the cry: "Down with Ripolin!" The reader should know that Ripolin is a prepared paint which anyone can apply, in order to understand the full sincerity of this slogan as well as its artlessness. Ripolin here represents injustice and oppression. It is the enemy, the devil. We all have our ripolin with which we colour, according to our needs, the abstract ideas which otherwise would be of no personal use to us.

It is under one of these motleys that the idea of liberty is presented to us by the politicians. Hearing this word, we now perceive little other than the idea of political liberty, and it would seem as if all the liberties which man is capable of enjoying were summed up in this ambiguous expression. Moreover, it is the same with the pure idea of liberty, as with the pure idea of justice; it is of no use to us in the ordinary business of life. Neither man nor nature is free, any more than either is just. Reasoning has no hold upon such ideas. To express them is to assert them, but they would necessarily falsify every argument into which one might wish to introduce them. Reduced to its social significance, the idea of liberty is still incompletely disassociated. There is no general idea of liberty, and it is difficult to form one, since the liberty of an individual is exercised only at the expense of the liberty of others. Formerly liberty was called privilege. Taking everything into account, that is perhaps its true name. Even today one of our relative liberties—the liberty of the press—is an ensemble of privileges. Privileges also are the liberty of speech granted to lawyers, the liberty of trade unions, and, tomorrow, the liberty of association as it is now proposed to us. The idea of liberty is perhaps only an emphatic corruption of the idea of privilege. The Latins, who made great use of the word liberty, meant by it the privilege of the Roman citizen.

It is seen that there is often an enormous gap between the common meaning of a word and its real significance in the depths of obscure verbal consciousnesses, whether because several associated ideas are expressed by a single word, or because the primitive idea has been submerged by the invasion of a secondary idea. It is thus possible—especially in dealing with generalizations—to write sentences having at once an apparent and a secret meaning. Words, which are signs, are almost always ciphers as well. The unconscious conventional language is very much in use, and there are even matters where it is the only one employed. But cipher implies deciphering. It is not easy to understand even the sincerest writing, and the author himself often goes astray because the meaning of words varies not only from one man to another, but from moment to moment, in the case of the same man. Language is thus a great cause of deception. It evolves in abstraction, while life evolves in complete concrete reality. Between speech and the things designated by speech, there is the same distance as between a landscape and the description of a landscape. And it must still further be borne in mind that the landscapes which we depict are known to us, most often, only through words which are, in turn, reflections of anterior words. Yet we understand each other. It is a miracle which I have no intention of analyzing at present. It will be more to our purpose, in concluding this sketch, which is merely a method, to undertake the examination of the quite modern ideas of art and of beauty.

I am ignorant of their origins, but they are later than the classic languages, which possess no fixed and precise words to express them, though the ancients were as well able as we to enjoy the reality they contain—better, even. They are intertangled. The idea of art is dependent upon the idea of beauty; but this latter idea is itself nothing but the idea of harmony, and the idea of harmony reduces itself to the idea of logic. The beautiful is that which is in its place. Thence arise the sentiments of pleasure given us by beauty. Or rather, beauty is a logic which is perceived as a pleasure. If this be admitted, it will at once be understood why the idea of beauty, in societies dominated by women, is almost always restricted to the idea of feminine beauty. Beauty is a woman. There is in this an interesting subject for analysis, but the question is somewhat complicated. It would be necessary to show, first, that woman is no more beautiful than man; that, situated on the same plane in nature, constructed on the same model, made of the same flesh, she would appear to a sensitive intelligence, exterior to humanity, exactly the female of man—exactly what, for man, a jenny is to a jack. And, observing them more closely, the Martian, who wished to learn something concerning the aesthetics of terrestrial forms, would even note that, if there be a real difference in beauty between a man and a woman of the same race, of the same caste, and of the same age, this difference is almost always in favour of the man; and that, moreover, if neither the man nor the woman be entirely beautiful, the defects of the human race are more accentuated in the woman, where the twofold projection of the belly and the buttocks—sexual attractions, no doubt—breaks unpleasantly the double line of the silhouette. The curve of the breasts is almost inflected under the influence of the back, which has a hollow tendency. Cranach's nudes confess naïvely these eternal imperfections of woman. Another defect which artists, when they have taste, remedy instinctively, is the shortness of the legs, so marked in the photographs of nude women. This cold anatomy of feminine beauty has often been made. It is, then, useless to insist upon it—all the more because, unfortunately, its verification is only too easy. But if woman's beauty be so vulnerable to criticism, how does it happen that, in spite of all, it remains indisputable—that it has become for us the very basis and leaven of the idea of beauty? It is a sexual illusion. The idea of beauty is not a pure idea. It is intimately connected with the idea of carnal pleasure. Stendhal had an obscure perception of this line of reasoning when he defined beauty as "a promise of happiness." Beauty is a woman, even for women themselves, who have carried docility with regard to men to the point of adopting this aphorism which they are capable of understanding only under the form of extreme sensual perversion. We know, however, that women have a particular type of beauty, which men have naturally branded "doll-like." If women were sincere, they would long ago have stigmatized equally the type of feminine beauty by which man most readily lets himself be seduced.

This identification of woman and beauty goes so far today that we have had innocently proposed us the "apotheosis of woman," meaning the glorification of beauty, with all the promises contained in Stendhal's definition taken in its erotic sense. Beauty is a woman and woman is a beauty. The caricaturists accentuate the common sentiment by invariably coupling with a woman, whom they strive to render beautiful, a man whose ugliness they stress to the extreme of vulgarity; and this in spite of the fact that pretty women are so rare in life, that after thirty a woman is almost always inferior, age for age, in plastic beauty, to her husband or lover. It is true that this inferiority is no easier to demonstrate than it is to feel, and that reasoning remains ineffective, once the page is finished, for the reader as well as for the writer; and this is very fortunate.

The idea of beauty has never been disassociated save by aestheticians. The common run of men accept Stendhal's definition, which amounts to saying that this idea does not exist—that it has been absolutely devoured by the idea of happiness—of sexual happiness, happiness given by a woman. That is why the cult of beauty is suspect for moralists who have analyzed the value of certain abstract words. They translate this one by the cult of the flesh, and they would be right, if that last expression did not imply a somewhat silly attack upon one of man's most natural tendencies. The necessary result has been that, in opposing such excessive apotheosis of woman, they have infringed upon the rights of art. Art being the expression of beauty, and it being possible to understand beauty only under the material aspects of the true idea which it contains, art has become almost uniquely feminine. Beauty is woman; and art, also, is woman. But the latter is less absolute. The notion of art is even fairly clear for artists and for the *élite*. The idea of art has been extremely well liberated. There is a pure art which is concerned exclusively with self-realization. No definition of it even should be given; for such a definition could not be made without connecting the idea of art with ideas which are foreign to it, and which would tend to obscure and sully it.

Previous to this disassociation, which is recent, and whose origin is known, the idea of art was connected with diverse ideas which are normally foreign to it—ideas of morality, of utility, or education. Art was the edifying illustration introduced into religious or philosophical catechism. This was the conception of the last two centuries. We freed ourselves from that yoke. There are now those who would like to put it back upon our necks. The idea of art has again been sullied, this time with the idea of utility. Art is called social by modern preachers. It is also called democratic, both epithets being well chosen, if it was meant by them to imply complete negation of its principal function. Admitting art because it can improve individuals or the masses, is like admitting roses because an eye-wash can be extracted from them. It is confounding two series of notions which the well-regulated exercise of the intelligence places upon entirely different planes. The plastic arts have a language; but this language cannot be translated into words and phrases. The work of art says things which are addressed directly to the aesthetic sense, and to it alone. What it can add, in such a way as to be understood by our other, faculties, is not worth listening to. And yet it is this negligible element which interests the boosters of social art. They are the majority and, as we are governed by the law of numbers, their triumph seems assured. The idea of art will, perhaps, prove to have been disassociated for a few years only, and for a small group of intelligences.

There are, then, a very large number of ideas that are never employed by men in their pure state, either because they have not yet been disassociated, or because this disassociation has been incapable of achieving stability. There are also a great many ideas which exist in the state of disassociation, or that can provisionally be considered so to exist, but which have a special affinity for other ideas with which they are most commonly encountered. There are still others which seem refractory to certain associations, whereas the facts to which they correspond are, in reality, extremely frequent. Here are a few examples of these affinities and of these repulsions, chosen in the profoundly interesting realm of commonplaces, or truths.

Flags were originally religious tokens, like the oriflamme of Saint-Denis, and their symbolic utility has remained at least as great as their real usefulness. But how, outside of war, have they become symbols of the idea of country? This is easier to explain by the facts themselves than by abstract logic. Today, in nearly all civilized countries, the idea of country and the idea of flag are invincibly associated. The two words are even interchangeable. But this is a question of symbolism quite as much as of association of ideas. Insistence upon it would lead us to the language of colours, counterpart of the language of flowers, but still more unstable and arbitrary. If it is amusing to note that the blue of the French flag is the consecrated colour of the Virgin and of the children of Mary, it is no less so to find that the pious purple of the robe of Saint-Denis has become a revolutionary symbol. Like the atoms of Epicurus, ideas cling together as best they may, through chance encounters, shocks and accidents.

Certain associations, though very recent, have rapidly acquired a singular authority, like those of education and intelligence, of education and morality. But, at most, education may have something to say for one of the particular forms of memory, or for a literal knowledge of the commonplaces contained in the Decalogue. The absurdity of these forced relations appears very clearly in that which concerns woman. It seems clear that there is a certain sort of education—that which they receive to-day—which, far from stimulating their intelligence, tends rather to blunt it. Since they have been educated seriously, they no longer have the least influence either in politics or in literature. Compare, in this connection, our last thirty years with the last thirty years of the *ancien régime*. These two associations of ideas have, nevertheless, become veritable commonplaces—truths which it is as useless to expose as to combat. They take their place with all those which infest books and the degenerate lobes of man's brain—with old and venerable truths like: virtue-recompense, vice-punishment, God-goodness, crime-remorse, duty-happiness, authority-respect, unhappiness-punishment, future-progress, and thousands of others, some of which, though absurd, are useful to mankind.

It would be equally possible to make a long catalogue of the ideas which men refuse to associate, while delighting in the most disconcerting *débauches*. We have given above the explanation of this stubborn attitude, namely, that their principal occupation is the pursuit of happiness, and that they are much more concerned with reasoning in accordance with their interests than with the rules of logic.

Thence the universal aversion to connecting the idea of nothingness with the idea of death. Though the former is evidently contained in the latter, humanity insists upon considering them separately. It opposes their union with all its force, never tiring of driving between them a chimerical wedge upon which resound the hammer-blows of hope. This is the finest example of the illogical that we can offer ourselves for our diversion, and the best proof that, in the gravest matters, as in those of slightest concern, it is sentiment which always triumphs over reason.

Is it a great thing to have learned that? Perhaps.

NOVEMBER, 1899.

Glory and the Idea of Immortality

I

The idea of glory is not one of the most difficult to resolve. It can be identified with the general idea of immortality, of which it is but one of the secondary and naïver forms, differing from it only in the substitution of vanity for pride. In the one we have the idea of duration fortified by the pride of a being who believes himself of immortal importance, but who consents to enjoy without fuss an absolute perennity. In the other, vanity, replacing pride, puts aside the idea of the absolute, or, declaring itself incapable of attaining it, clings to a desire of eternity, no doubt, but an objective eternity, perceptible to others—a ceremonial eternity which wastes in world-wide repute that which absolute immortality gains in depth and in proud humility.

Abstract words define inadequately an abstract idea. It is better to fall back upon the common opinion. Everybody knows what glory is. Every writer pictures to himself literary glory. Nothing is clearer than this sort of illusion. Nothing is clearer than love and desire. Definitions, which are indispensable for dictionaries only, contain of reality precisely what a net, raised at the wrong moment from the sea where it awaited its prey, contains of obscure, squirming life. Sea-weed writhes in its meshes. Lanky creatures stir their translucent claws, and here are all sorts of helices or of valvules which a mechanical sensibility keeps tight-shut. But reality, which was a big fish, with a sudden swish of its tail, flopped overboard. Generally speaking, clear, neat sentences have no meaning. They are affirmative gestures, suggesting obedience, and that is all. The human mind is so complex, and things are so tangled up in each other that, in order to explain a blade of grass, the entire universe would have to be taken to pieces; and in no language is there a single authentic word upon which a lucid intelligence could not construct a psychological treatise, a history of the world, a novel, a poem, a drama, according to the day and the temperature. The definition is a sack of compressed flour contained in a thimble. What can we do with it, unless we are antarctic explorers? It is more to the point to place a pinch of flour under the microscope and seek patiently, amid the bran, the living starch. In what is left after analyzing the idea of immortality, the idea of glory will be found a shining speck of gold.

Man still believes himself the last achievement of the creative power. Darwin, corroborating the Bible, ushered the human couple out of the shades on the sixth day only; and the leading scientists take the same stand—a fact which favours those dubious books in which the questionable concordance of Science and Faith is celebrated. But Darwinism is on the eve of disappearing before preciser notions. Tomorrow we shall no longer be obliged to believe that the creator of the universe, having organized the lower species without moral ideas, invented man for the purpose of depositing in his brain a principle which it had got along very well without itself, in the course of its preparatory labours. If man is no longer the latest arrival,—if he is a very old animal in the history of life,—if the flower of the life-tree is not Adam but the Dove,—then the whole metaphysic of morals will collapse. What! after the masterpiece, Man, He (or She, according to which meaningless word may be professed) humbles Himself to make the Bird! What! the stork after

Abraham's ancestor! Yet so it is. M. Quinton's labours[1] will no longer permit us to doubt it. It becomes certain that the human intelligence, far from being the goal of creation, is only an accident, and that moral ideas are but parasitic vegetations arising from an excess of nutrition. The phenomena of intelligence, moral consciousness, and all the titles of nobility engrossed on the parchment, might perfectly well, no doubt, have appeared in any other species whatsoever. The birds, whose evolution is as yet incomplete, will not, perhaps, be exempted from them. Their arterial system is superior to man's—simpler and stronger. They can eat without interrupting their breathing. They steal,

---

[1] *Communication à l'Académie des Sciences (13 Avril 1896)*, certified and rendered more precise by later investigations which M. Quinton has explained to me. Here, without scientific apparatus, is what, as a result of precious conservations, would appear to be the general order in which the animals appeared, beginning with the fishes, and taking account only of those which have yet been covered:

I. Fish			IV. Mammals	V. Birds
II. Batracians	a.	Monotrema	x. Primates	
III. Reptiles	b.	Marsupials	(Lemurs, Mon-	
	c.	Edentates	keys, Men)	
	d.	Rodents	y. Carnivora (latest	
	e.	Insectivora	arrivals: blue fox,	
	f.	-- -- --	white bear)	
	g.	-- -- --	z. Ruminants (last	
	h.	-- -- --	arrival: reindeer)	
		-- -- --		
		-- -- --		

The bearing of this list upon any question whatsoever of general philosophy is evident for all who know how to disassociate ideas. It would have thrilled Voltaire. For the rest, I claim the honour of having been the first to announce to the larger public these new scientific views, which will, logically, have a magnificent wealth of consequences. I have already made a less precise allusion to them, notably in the *Wiener Rundschau*, May 1899.

they speak, they can recite the Rights of Man or the Nicene Creed—supreme achievements of large numbers of men. The bird, chronological king of creation, has remained, till now, and in spite of its improvements, an animal. The bird series does not seem, in point of intelligence, superior to that of the mammals, among which Man figures as an inexplicable exception. Intelligence could then be regarded as an end, only if each of the animal species were rigorously determined and stationary. This is M. Quinton's opinion, at least provisionally. The species, since they are species—since the individuals which compose them are reproduced in beings identical with themselves—the species, such as they are defined, by these very syllables—species—may disappear, but they can no longer change. Man has quite certainly passed through various states in which he was not a man; but the day man produced a man, humanity began immutable. It is then possible that human intelligence, instead of being an accident, a derogation, was determined, from the beginning, like the human hand, the human feet, the human hair. It would then have a normal, logical rôle in the universe, and its very excess—genius—would be but exuberance of energy. But we should still have to explain the bird's stupidity. Is it, perhaps, an evidence of the intellectual degeneration of the creative forces? The most probable opinion is that intelligence is an excrescence, like an oak-apple. To what insect's bite do we owe it? We shall never know.

It matters little whether the intelligence be, as Taine believed, a normal product of the brain, or a malady, especially as a blemish, transmitted as such from generation to generation, ends by losing its pathological characteristics. It becomes an integral and normal part of the organism.[2] Its accidental

---

2 Intelligence can thus be conceived as an initial form of instinct, in which case the human intelligence would be destined to crystallize into instinct, as has occurred in the case of other animal species. Consciousness would disappear, leaving complete liberty to the unconscious act,

origin is, however, corroborated by this, that although an excellent instrument for a priori combinations, the intelligence is, one would say, especially unfitted for the perception of realities. It is to this infirmity that we owe metaphysics, religions and ethical systems. As the external world can reach the consciousness only by scrupulously conforming to all the nooks and crannies of the pocket, it turns out that, believing to hold an image of the world, we have only an image of ourselves. Certain rectifications are possible. Analysis of the phenomena of vision has made us admit that. By comparing our sensations and our ideas with what we can comprehend of the sensations and ideas of others, we arrive at a determination of probable averages; but, above all, negative averages. It would be easier to draw up a list of non-truths than a list of truths. To affirm that a given religion is false, no longer denotes great boldness of intellect or even much intellect. The veracity of any religion whatsoever is today a subject for controversy only for the various European clergies who make their living out of it, or for those belated rationalists who, like their master Kant, are ever awaiting the propitious and lucrative hour for opportune conversions. But, to the naïve question presented by those who, like nature, in the seventeenth century, abhor a vacuum:—"What will you put in its place?"—no answer can be made. It is enough, and it is no small thing at that, to have transmuted a truth into a non-truth. The higher calling of criticism is not even, as Pierre Bayle proclaimed, to sow doubts; it must destroy. The intelligence is an excellent instrument of negation. It is time to employ it, and so stop trying to rear palaces with picks and torches.

The history of the idea of immortality is a good example of our congenital inability to perceive realities otherwise than reshaped and worked over by the understanding. The idea of

---

necessarily perfect in the limits of its intention. The conscious man is a scholar who will reveal himself a master the moment he has become a delicate but unerring machine, like bee and beaver.

immortality is born of belief in the double. In sleep, and while the body is inert, there is a part of man that stirs, that travels, that fights, that eats, enjoys or suffers, exhibits all the phenomena of life. This part of man, this double of man, this astral body, survives the decomposition of the material body, whose habits and needs it keeps. Such, doubtless, is the origin of the belief in what, since Hellenism, we call the immortality of the soul. In an earlier stage, the Egyptian religion was based upon the theory of the double. It was for doubles, and not for souls, that first real, and later symbolic, food was placed in the tombs. But the Egyptian religion was already charged, in addition, with the idea of justice, of equilibrium. The doubles were weighed in the scales of good and evil. Ethical metaphysics had obscured the primitive idea of immortality, which is nothing but the idea of indefinite duration.

For theologians, for philosophers—if there still be any to profess these honest doctrines—for the common run of men, the idea of immortality, or of the future life, is intimately connected with the idea of justice. Eternal happiness is a compensation accorded human sorrows. There are also—but these are for theologians only—personal torments to punish infractions of priestly orders, which tortures are, moreover, an additional recompense for the good, and a guarantee against promiscuity. We have here an aristocratic selection, but one based upon the idea of good and bad, instead of upon that of strength and weakness. These strange reversals of values enraged Nietzsche. They should be accepted as at least transitory consequences of civilized man's sensibility. Primitive man, whose nervous vibrations are few, and whose intelligence is passive, feels suffering, though dully, but does not feel injustice, which is moral suffering. To encounter a similar state we must cross the middle regions, and question a Goethe, a Taine or a Nietzsche—men in whom intelligence has finally conquered by its very excess, repelling the pleadings of pity and the sentimental pitfalls of justice. If the idea of immortality had been born in a superior intelligence, it would have differed only by its greater logic from the brutal conceptions of primitive humanity.

M. Marillier has collected and co-ordinated all that which, in the beliefs of the uncivilized, relates to the survival of the soul.[3] The ensemble of the facts shows that the idea of justice has had not the slightest share in forming the conception of the idea of immortality. There have been few discoveries more important for the history of human beliefs. The idea of immortality was, at first, as M. Marillier has the hardihood to assert, a purely scientific conception. It is the magnification and prolongation of a fact—of a fact badly observed, but still a fact. The future life is the continuation of the present life, and involves the same customs, the same pleasures, the same annoyances. This world also has a double: the other world. The bad and the good, the strong and the weak, continue there as here. Sometimes life, without change in the relations of its elements, is more clement in the other world. Sometimes, in the same conditions, it is worse. But, whether the future life be considered as better or worse, it is the same for all. Better still, it implies perfect equality in those commonplace pleasures which are the average ideal of the civilized man as well as of the savage. The tribes of New Guinea, rendered anaemic by hunger, dream of eating unlimited sago throughout eternity. As it would be possible to discover, even in this egalitarian paradise, some vague idea of compensation, hence of justice; we must go farther, to Java, where paradise—doubtless because of an excessive toll—was accessible only to the rich; to those resigned races, where alone the kings, the priest and the nobles, were saved; to Borneo, where the hereafter, divided into seven circles, corresponded to the seven circles of the social hierarchy. In another corner of

---

3 *La Survivance de l'Ame et l'idée de justice chez les peuples non civilisés*, Paris, Leroux, 1894.

the great island, "every person whom a man kills in this world becomes his slave in the next." There we have a paradise clearly based upon the idea of force, and a belief which laughs a little at the categorical imperative. Not only is the weak not "recompensed," but his weakness and his suffering may, through the caprice of the strong, be raised to the infinite. The slayer has acquired an immortal profit. Societies in which there is poetry, art, laughter, love, still exist with such a morality. The fact may sadden, but it does not surprise us; for it is evident that we have here a terrible element of resistance against foreigners. Such a system has its drawbacks. From time to time, in Borneo, a band of young Dyaks who have not yet killed, dash into a town and slay. Having thus gained immortal life and a slave, they remain more tranquil thereafter. Among the Shans, a man killed by an elephant forfeits paradise. Eaten by a tiger, he becomes a tiger. Women who die in child-bed become ghouls and haunt the tombs, their feet reversed, heels foremost. In the Mariannas, there is a heaven and a hell. Violent death leads to hell, natural death to paradise. These people were destined to be slaves from all eternity. In another region of Oceania, the fate of the soul is decided by the family of the deceased, who throw dice for it. Odd means annihilation, even eternal happiness. In Tahiti, the blind souls, on leaving the body, wander away to a plain where there are two stones. One, touched first, confers immortal life, the other eternal death. This is almost sublimely absurd. It is as grandiose and terrible as predestination. Saint Augustine placed the one in the night, before birth. The Tahitians situated the other in the shades, after death. Protestantism, to which those poor people have since surrendered, has not much changed their beliefs. Generally speaking, the greatest effort of a religious or philosophical innovator is to put at the end what was originally at the beginning, or vice versa.

By connecting itself with the idea of immortality, the idea of justice has, then, singularly disturbed its original character.

It has even contaminated the idea of earthly immortality—the idea of glory.

II

How glory, first reserved for the kings and warriors sung by the poets, has come finally to be attributed to the poets themselves, even more than to the heroes of their poems, is an historic fact whose exact origin would be of little interest. It would be more curious to discover as a result of what change in the manners and customs, or through what enhancement of egoism and of vanity, the complicated idea of justice came to attach itself to the idea of the perennity of the name and of the work. At what epoch of Greek civilization, did an Athenian dramatist, whose play had been flouted by the public, have the boldness to appeal to posterity? Are any ancient texts known wherein such recriminations may be read? Sensibility has increased to such an extent that there exists today no scorned poetaster who does not dream of the justice of future generations. The *exigi monumentum* of Horace and Malherbe has become democratized; but how can we believe that the vanity of authors has ever had a beginning? The fact must be admitted, however, in order to keep within the logic of the successive developments of human character.

Literary glory was at first merely the sentiment of the future duration of the present reputation—a legitimate sentiment which accords fairly well with the facts; for absolute revivals are almost as rare as solid rehabilitations. Today it is a scientific probability. Æschylus believed that the relation existing in his own lifetime between the *Suppliants* and public opinion would continue the same throughout the ages. Æschylus was right; but not if he cherished the same dream with regard to the *Danaides* and the *Egyptians*. Yet Pratinas saw himself, in the future, one of the rivals of Æschylus, and Pratinas is today but a word, scarcely a name. The idea of glory, even in its oldest and most legitimate form, would seem, therefore, to contain the idea of justice, at least by preterition, since its non-realization at once suggests to us the idea of injustice. But men of so ancient a civilization should not be made to reason in terms of our modern sensibility. Pratinas would, perhaps, have submitted to destiny. He would, perhaps, have called a fact, pure and simple, what we are pleased to name injustice.

The idea of justice, since it is subject, to the variations of sensibility, is of the most instable sort. Most of the facts that we class today in the category of injustice, were left by the Greeks in the category of destiny. For others, which we ditch under the name of misfortune, or of fatality, they strove to find a cure. In principle, when a people restricts the category "destiny" in favour of the category "injustice," the truth has begun to confess its decadence. The extreme state of sensibility to injustice is symbolized by the gag of Zaina, who breathed only through a veil, in order to destroy no life—a state of intellectual degradation towards which European humanity, with its mystic vegetarians, precursors of sentimental socialists, is also progressing today. Have we not already our "lower brothers," and are we not agreed to praise the machines that spare animals the exercise of their muscles? To weep over the slave who turns the wheel, or the poet who sings in the desert, is a sign of depravity; for the fact is that the slave who turns the wheel loves life more than he suffers from his labour, while the poet who croaks like a frog in his hole finds singing an agreeable physiological exercise.

The physical laws promulgated or established by scientists are confessions of ignorance. When they cannot explain a mechanism, they declare that its movements are due to a law. Bodies fall by virtue of the law of gravitation. This has precisely the same value, in the serious order, as the comic *virtus dormitiva*. Categories are confessions of impotence. To throw a fact into the abyss of destiny, or into the drawer of injustice, is to renounce the exercise of the most natural analytical faculties. The *Lusiads* was saved because Camoens was a good swimmer, and Newton's treatise on light and colours was lost because his little dog, Diamond, overturned a candle. Presented thus, these two events belong henceforth neither in the category Providence nor in the category Fatality. They are simple facts—facts like thousands of others that have occurred without men finding in them a pretext for enthusiasm or for anger. That Æschylus has survived and Pratinas is dead are accidents like those which happen in war. There are some more scandalous, but none should be judged in accordance with the puerile notion of a distributive justice. If justice is wounded because Florus keeps afloat in the shipwreck where Varius and Calvus perish, it is justice which is wrong. It was out of place there.

However, just as it has attached itself to the idea of paradise, so the idea of justice has become the parasite of the idea of glory. For the immortality for which Tahiti gambled heads or tails, has, with the best will in the world, been substituted providential immortality; but, so far as glory, at any rate, is concerned, we know that Providence, even if it does not determine the name of the elect by lot, is governed by motives that it would, perhaps, not dare to acknowledge. However unjust man may be, by nature and by taste, he is less unjust than the God he has created. Thus, as Ausonius has pertinently remarked, chaste men engender obscene literatures. So, also, the work of the veritable genius is always inferior to the brain which bore it. Civilization has put a little method into glory, provisionally.

Even in the spiritual order, men have almost always been at variance with the decisions of their gods. Most of the saints in the past were created by the people in spite of the priests. In the course of the centuries the catalogue of the saints and the catalogue of the great men have drawn so far apart that they will soon not have a single name in common. Almost all the really venerable men of this last century—almost all those whose clay contained veins or traces of gold—were outcasts. We live in the age of Prometheus. When Providence alone ruled the earth, during the interregnum of humanity, she caused such hecatombs that intelligence nearly perished. In the year 950, the son of a serf of Aurillac, young Gerbert, summed up almost the whole European tradition. He was, all by himself, civilization. What a moment in history! Men, by an admirable instinct, made him their master. He was Pope Sylvester II. When he died, there began to be built, on that column which had sustained the world, the legend destined to find its culmination in Goethe's *Faust*. Such is Glory, that Gerbert is unknown. But he is not unknown like Pythagoras. It has been possible to write his life, his writings have been preserved. If Gerbert is not one of our great men today, he will perhaps be tomorrow. He has kept intact all the possibilities of his resurrection. The reason is that, leaving aside the paradoxical idea of Providence, we have since Gerbert scarcely changed our civilization.

When the Christians came into power, they preserved, outside those few spared by chance, only the books necessary for school instruction. There has survived of Antiquity precisely what would have survived of the seventeenth century, if the professors of the old University, together with the Jesuits and the Minims, had possessed the power of life and death over books. Adding La Fontaine to Boileau's catalogue, they would have burned the rest. The Christians burned much, in spite of their professions of love; and what they did not burn they expurgated. It is to them that we owe the almost burlesque image of a chaste Virgil. The authentic incompletion of the *Æneid* afforded a good pretext for cuts and erasures. The booksellers charged with the task were, moreover, unintelligent and lazy. But the great cause of the disappearance of almost all pagan literature was more general. A day came when it was deemed of no interest. From the first centuries its circle had already begun to dwindle. Could a Saint Cecilia find any pleasure in Gallus? This delicious, heroic Roman woman (who was found last century lying in the dust, in her bloody robes) changed her heart with her religion. Women ceased to read Gallus, and Gallus has almost completely perished.

In his interesting book on this subject,[4] M. Stapfer has not taken into account changes in civilization. He has thought only of chance to explain the loss of so many ancient books. Chance is a mask, and it is precisely the duty of the historian to lift this mask, or to tear it. Between the sixth century and our own day, there has been one further partial modification in civilization—in the fifteenth century. About that time, the old literature began to lose its hold upon the public. The novels, the miracles, the tales seemed suddenly to have aged. They were no longer copied or recited. They were seldom printed, a single manuscript having preserved for us *Aucassin et Nicolette,* which is something like the *Daphnis and Chloe* of the Middle Ages. Accidents frighten the poet—and even the critic, who is colder, whose logic is more rigorous—the moment the suggestion is made of separating the purely historical idea of literary survival from the sentimental idea of justice. Till now—and I allude once more to the conservative rôle of modern civilization—the printing-press has protected writers against destruction; but the serious rôle of printing affects as yet only four centuries. This distant invention will appear some day as if contemporary at once with Rabelais and with Victor Hugo. When a time equal to that which separates us from the birth of Æschylus—two thousand three hundred and seventy-five years, let us say—shall have elapsed between us and a given moment of the future, what influence will printing have had on the preservation of

---

4 *Des Réputations littéraires: Essai de morale et d'histoire.* Première série. Paris, Hachette, 1893.

books? Perhaps none. Everything not worth the trouble of reprinting—that is to say everything, with the exception of a few fortunate fragments—will have disappeared, and the more rapidly that the material substance of books has become more precarious. Even the discovery of a durable paper would not give absolute assurance of survival, because of the temptation to employ this excessively strong paper for a thousand other purposes. Thus the value of the parchment has often led to the sacrifice of a manuscript, just as gold articles go necessarily to the smelting-pot once the style has changed. The best material for the preservation of books would be something unchanging, but fragile, slightly brittle, so that it would be good for nothing outside its binding. Would not such a discovery be a curse?

For the work of the last four centuries, and for what, about 1450, remained undamaged of the earlier work, as well as for what has since been found in the dustbins, printing has proved a memorable blessing. We are not obliged to accept the opinions of the past. The books are there, and whether they be common or rare, we can find and read them. We are the startled and clement judges of the glory and of the obloquy that Boileau distributed to his contemporaries. Martial dishonoured poets who were perhaps a Saint Amant or a Scudéry; but we have beneath our eyes the documents composing the *dossier* of the *Satires,* and no professor friendly to good morals and eternal principles can make us share his commonplace hatreds. A witty writer has remarked that Boileau treated the writers whom he disliked almost the way we treat convicted assassins or seducers of little girls; but, thanks to the unforeseen permanence of books, this ancient abuse matters no more for the judges today than a lawyer's vituperation. I have Sanlecque within hand's reach, even Cotin, even Coras. If they are poor writers, I shall say so only as a result of my own personal impression.

A catalogue of lost books has been compiled.[5] Their number reaches five or six hundred, and to attain even this figure, the author was obliged to count some works which have merely strayed, as well as several editions of works reprinted more than once. Were there, among these lost books, any pages really worth crying over? It is hardly likely, judging from the epitaphs of these tombs. The following were doubtless neither other *Maximes,* nor other *Phèdres,* nor even other *Alarics: Herménégilde,* tragedy, by Gaspard Olivier (1601); the *Poétiques Trophées,* by Jean Figon de Montélimard (1556), or the *Courtisan Amoureux* (1582) or the *Friant Dessert des Femmes mondaines* (1643). But who knows? However, the *Coupe-Cul des Moines,* or the *Seringue spirituelle,* inspires but feeble regrets, and it is the same with the *Estranges et espouvantables Amours d'un diable déguisé en gentil-homme et d'une demoiselle de Bretagne.* A more palpable loss is that of several *Almanachs* prepared by Rabelais, but even this does not matter so very much. The fact that feverish fingers wore out the first editions of *Astrée,* of the *Aventures du baron de Fœneste,* of the *Odes* of Ronsard prematurely,[6] proves nothing but the immediate success of these works which do not cease to be in the hands of all connoisseurs for more than half a century, and the same might be said of the original editions of the first novels of Alexandre Dumas, which cannot be classed, for the most part, among lost books. But the fact that we can still read the inscriptions in a cemetery proves, at least, that those buried beneath them had a name and a fame, however transitory. The real lost books are those whose very titles today could be suspected by nobody. This anonymous dust would not, doubtless, fill a very large ossuary; but a necropolis could be constructed from lost manuscripts.

---

5 *Livres perdus: Essai bibliographique sur les livres devenus introuvables,* by Philoumeste Junior, Brussels, 1882.
6 These privately printed editions of three hundred copies or less have necessarily been worn out in proportion to their success.

It is not probable that, of the French literature of the Middle Ages, much more than the hundredth part has survived the changing fashion. Almost all the dramatic works have disappeared. The number of authors must have been immense at a time when the writer was his own publisher, the poet his own reciter, the dramatist his own actor. In a certain sense printing proved an obstacle to letters. It operated a selection and cast contempt upon books that had failed to find a publisher. This situation still exists, though mitigated by the low cost of mechanical typography. The invention with which we are now threatened—a home-printing-press—would triple or quadruple the number of new books, and we should have mediaeval conditions once more. Everyone with a smattering of culture—and some others, as is the case today—would venture the little work which the writer confides to his friends before offering it to the public. Every progress ends by defeating its own purpose. Reaching its maximum development, it tends to re-establish the primitive state which it had superseded.

The change in civilization, from antiquity to the Middle Ages, was intellectual and sentimental rather than material. The same trades continued under the same primitive conditions. The bookshop in the time of Rutebeuf was the same that sold the *Odes* of Horace, when they were fresh and full of life. In both periods, which were similarly periods of expansion, literature was similarly abundant. There remains almost nothing of it today. All Latin poetry, from Ennius to Sidonius Apollinaris, is contained in two folio volumes,[7] but almost the whole second volume is devoted to the Christian poets. The Greeks have been less badly treated. Antony made a gift to Cleopatra of the library at Pergamos, which contained two hundred thousand Greek works, each in a single copy. Greek literature, in Didot's edition, is contained in sixty-one volumes. If we add

---

7 *Opera et Fragmenta veterorum poetarum latinorum.* London, 1713.

an occasional treatise of Aristotle, Herondas, Bacchylides, the number of pages will not be greatly increased. Literature fared the same as an army which has been decimated. The dead are buried and the survivors become heroes. We may judge of the relative, but not of the absolute value of what is left. Here we encounter Pratinas once more. He teaches us that glory is a fact.

III

Glory is a fact pure and simple, and not a fact of justice. There is no exact relation between the real merit of a writer (our examination is limited to literary glory) and his standing. In order to reward the survival of the book during the last four hundred years, in accordance with the dictates of chance and, if you like, of injustice, criticism has invented a hierarchal system which divides writers into castes, from the idiot to the man of genius. This looks solid and serious. It is, however, arbitrary, since aesthetic or moral judgments are merely generalized sensations. Literary judgment thus rejoins religious judgment so completely as to become identified with it.

Earthly immortality and the other—that which operates ideally beyond real life—are conceptions of the same order, due to a single cause—the impossibility for thought to think of itself as non-existent. Descartes merely presented a physiological maxim whose human truth is so absolute that it would have been understood by the oldest and humblest peoples. "I think, therefore I am," is the verbal translation of a cellular state. Every living brain thinks this, even though unconsciously. Each minute of life is an eternity. It has neither beginning nor end. It is what it is. It is absolute. Yet the disagreement between the cerebral truth and the material truth is complete. The organ by which man thinks himself immortal dies, and the absolute is conquered by reality. The disagreement is complete, evident, undeniable. Yet it is inexplicable. Confronted with such a contradiction, the hypothesis of a duality assumes a certain force, besides which the laboratory itself affirms the essential difference between muscular and cerebral toil. The bending of the forearm, and even of a phalanx, releases a certain amount of carbonic acid. Cerebral activity, all muscles being in repose, registers no trace of combustion. This does not mean that the organs of thought are immaterial. They can be touched, weighed and measured; but their materiality is of a special sort whose vital reactions are as yet unknown. Inexplicable in theory, the disagreement between thought and the flesh is thus explained, in fact, by a difference at least of molecular construction. They are two states, each of which has but a superficial knowledge of the other, and the flesh which thought always represents to itself as eternal is certain of dissolution.

There are, then, two immortalities: the subjective immortality which a man accords himself readily, even necessarily, and the objective immortality, of which Pratinas has been robbed and which is a fact. If what we have said be true and if, in the absence of precise methods of analysis, the first—religious or literary—no longer admits of other than philosophic—that is to say, vague—reflections, objective immortality, on the other hand, is a less abstract subject for discussion. It would even be possible, with a little good will, to bring all history within its scope; but French literature forms a long and brilliant enough cavalcade for our purpose.

The moment words clasp beneath their wings a certain amount of perceptible reality, they readily yield their formula. Glory is life in the memory of men. But of what men, what life?

M. Stapfer[8] has attempted to enumerate the works which, from the sixteenth to the eighteenth century, have lasted—what is called "lasting" in professional critical language. This

---

8 Opus cit., p. 103.

chapter, wittily entitled (with a touch of Jansenism) "the little number of elect," would be brief were it but a catalogue. In short—and this may be admitted provisionally—among all the French writers of the last three centuries, twenty-five or thirty may be said to have achieved what is called glory; but of these thirty, the majority are scarcely more than a name. What life, and of what men? M. Stapfer is thinking of works that it might occur to a modern Frenchman, "of average culture," to glance at on a rainy day. It is impossible to make a serious analysis if we permit such expressions as "average culture" to enter our reasoning. A man of "average culture" may very possibly enjoy Saint-Simon, without owning either a Pascal, a Bossuet, a Corneille or a Malherbe. A man can read and reread Pascal, yet have little taste for Rabelais. But these amateurs of hard reading are professors, churchmen, lawyers—men who, even if they are not writers themselves, have a professional interest in letters, and are obliged to keep in touch with the classic period of French literature. And where have they learned that Boileau is a better poet than Théophile or Tristan? At college, for it is through the college that literary glory maintains itself in the bored recollection of heedless generations. There is no "average culture" that can be felt and figured by a flexible curve; but there are programmes. Villiers de l'Isle-Adam invented the "Glory Machine." There is, in the Ministry of Public Instruction, a hall on the door of which should be read: "Bureau of Glory." It is the seat of the Superior Council which elaborates the study programme. This programme is the "stuffer" which produces average cultures. Names omitted from it will remain eternally unknown to generations whose paternal guide it will be. But an educator's conscience will not permit him to impose upon children knowledge of writers whose morality is not universally admitted. Molière was very immoral in his day, and this was the secret of his success with a public which had no other choice, on its days of repentance, than among the most eloquent or the most skilful preachers. It is as he has been less understood, that Molière has become, little by little, a moralist. As successive sensibilities have distinguished themselves more sharply from the sensibility of the seventeenth century, the coarseness has lost its rank odour and we have come at last to find delicate certain sallies which, brought up to date, would embarrass us. Molière, much more brutal at bottom than on the surface, enjoys what might be called an acquired morality. It is an inevitable phenomenon of adjustment. It was necessary either to sacrifice Molière or to demonstrate the beauty of his philosophic genius.

His saying, which is only a saying, "For the love of humanity," has been hollowed and dug out by the commentators like an ivory ball which, at last, in the lathe, becomes a system of concentric spheres. It is merely a child's rattle. How are the *Femmes Savantes* and Feminism to be reconciled? This will be a very curious teat to follow. In her *Réflexions sur les Femmes,* so penetrating and so well written, Madame de Lambert says that this comedy, odious in itself, made education for young women seem improper, immodest, almost obscene; whence the craze for purely sensual pleasure to which women inclined, since they had no other resources than love and good living. The difficulty will be solved by considering separately the idea of feminism and the idea of the *Femmes Savantes,* and by cavilling at the word "savant," which has recently come to have a very definite significance. The *savant,* in the seventeenth century, was the amateur, not only of the sciences, but of letters—the man eager for all novelties, who discussed vortices without neglecting Vaugelas. Madame de Sévigné was a "femme savante," also Ninon. No doubt it was necessary to save Molière's work. It was worth it. But might not it have been done more honestly, and with greater lucidity?

Attempted on Rabelais and on Montaigne, the same work of adjustment has been less successful. Rabelais, in particular, has discouraged the most stubbornly naïve; and, since it was impossible to glean virtuous sheaves in his abbey of good pleasure, Pantagruel was classed among the vague precursors of modern ideas—which has no appreciable meaning, modern ideas being extremely contradictory. La Fontaine has lent himself to the caprices of the moralists with that indifference to good and evil which was the peculiarity of his exclusively sensual temperament; while, as for Racine, whose work would be frightful, were it not expressed in a language as cold and abstract as algebra, the Jansenist devotion of his last days has made it possible to discover pious intonations even in his most delirious celebrations of cruelty and lust.[9] Why has not the same process been applied to a Saint-Amant or a Théophile? Here is seen the influence of Boileau, whom it is still dangerous to contradict when seeking a certain quality of reputation. Happy to find their task limited and determined by a celebrated authority, the educators closed their catalogue of glories the moment it was decently long enough. Their enterprise was one of moral, far more than literary, criticism. A single book—the *Fables,* for example—would have sufficed them as an album wherein to deposit the cunning aphorisms of the old catechism. The educator's ideal is the *Koran,* whose pages contain, at the same time, a sample of writing, a model of style, a religious code, and a handbook of morals.

We may, then, conclude that, in reality, there is no literary glory. The great writers are offered to our admiration not as writers, but as moralists. Literary glory is an illusion.

And yet, in reserving for school-use some of the greatest French men of genius, the literary historians have been obliged

---

[9] This was written on the appearance of M. Louis Proal's work, *Le Crime et le Suicide Passionnels* (F. Alcan, 1910), in which, referring to sex dramas in the criminal courts, Racine is quoted, every ten pages, for reference and comparison. Everyone hesitates to say just what an age of passion and of carnal madness the *Grand Siècle* really was.

to justify their choice, to feign artistic preoccupations. Nisard wrote a history of French literature concerned with little else than morality. Such a preoccupation was found noble, but too exclusive. The common handbooks mingle adroitly the two orders. A child should not know quite whether La Fontaine is prescribed for him as a great poet or as an old chap who counselled prudence—as the author of *Philémon et Baucis,* or as the precursor of Franklin. Armed with the four rules of literature, the professors have examined talents and classified them. They have conferred prizes and honourable mentions. There is the first order and there are orders graduated all the way down to the fourth and the fifth. French literature has become arranged hierarchically like a tenement house. "Villon," one of these measurers once said to me, "is not of the first order." Admiration must be shaded according to the seven notes of the university scale. Earnest flutists excel at this game.

It is not a question of disputing the awards of glory or of proposing a revised list. Such as it is, it serves its purpose. It may have the same usefulness as the arbitrary classifications of botany. It is not a matter of amending it, it is a matter of tearing it up.

That Racine is a better poet than Tristan l'Hermite, and that *Iphigénie* is superior to *Marianne,* are two propositions unequally true; for we might quite as well be asked to compare this, which is by Racine:

> Que c'est une chose charmante
> De voir cet étang gracieux
> Où, comme en un lit précieux,
> L'onde est toujours calme et dormante!
>
> Quelles richesses admirables
> N'ont point ces nageurs marquetés,
> Ces poissons aux dos argentés,

> Sur leurs écailles agréables![10]

with this, which is by Tristan:

> Auprès de cette grotte sombre
> Où l'on respire un air si doux,
> L'onde lutte avec les cailloux,
> Et la lumière avec que l'ombre.
>
> Ces flots, las de l'exercice
> Qu'ils ont fait dessus ce gravier,
> Se reposent dans ce vivier,
> Où mourut autrefois Narcisse.
>
> L'ombre de cette fleur vermeille
> Et celle de ces jons pendans
> Paraissent estre la-dedans
> Les songes de l'eau qui someille.[11]

I am well aware that I am here comparing the best of Tristan with the worst of Racine; but all the same, if Racine had his park, Tristan had his garden, and it is often agreeable there. Let us then tear up the list of awards in order to remain ignorant of the fact that Tristan l'Hermite is a poet "whose versification is ridiculous,"[12] so that our pleasure in meeting him may not thus be spoiled in advance, and so that, with him, we may dare address his muse:

> Fay moy boire au creux de tes mains,
> Si l'eau n'en dissout point la neige.

This is the drawback to comparative methods. Having set up

---

10 *L'Étang*. This poem forms part of the set of five odes in which Racine celebrated Port-Royal des Champs: *L'Étang, Les Prairies, Les Bois, Les Troupeaux, Les Jardins*.
11 *Le Promenoir des Deux Amans*.
12 Vapereau, *Dictionnaire des Littératures*.

the great poet of the century as a standard, the critics thereafter value the others merely as precursors or as disciples.[13] Authors are often judged according to what they are not, through failure to understand their particular genius, and often also through failure to question them themselves. Pratinas, truly, is better treated. He enjoys silence.

But he is dead, and we are discussing the living. Living what life, and in the memory of what men? Life is a physical fact. A book which exists as a volume in a library is not dead, and is it not perhaps a glory more enviable to remain unknown, like Théophile, than to be famous, like Jean-Baptiste Rousseau? When glory is merely classic, it is perhaps one of the harshest forms of humiliation. To have dreamed of thrilling men and women with passion, and to become but the dull task which keeps the careless schoolboy a captive! Are there, however, any universal reputations that are not classic? Very few, and in that case, they have another blemish. It is for their smut that Restif's[14] ridiculous novels are still read—also Voltaire's syphilitic tales, and that tedious *Manon Lescaut,* so clumsily adapted from the English. The books of yesterday no longer have a public, if by public be understood disinterested men who read simply for their pleasure, enjoying the art and the thought contained in a book; but they still have readers, and all have some.

The only dead book is the book which is lost. All the rest live, almost with the same life, and the older they grow, the more intense this life becomes, becoming more precious. Literary glory is nominal. Literary life is personal. There is not a poet of the prodigious seventeenth century who does not come to life again each day in the pious hands of a lover. Bossuet has

---

13 An excellent doctor's thesis on Tristan l'Hermite, by M. V. M. Demadin, bears precisely this title: *Un précurseur de Racine.*
14 The first volume, and that alone, of Restif de la Bretonne's *Monsieur Nicholas* should be excepted.

not been more thumbed than this *Recueil* by Pierre du Marteu;[15] and, all things considered, the Plainte du cheval Pégase aux chevaux de la petite Écurie, by Monsieur de Benserade, is more agreeable and less dangerous reading than the *Discours sur l'Histoire Universelle*. Is pompous moralizing after all so superior to sprightly burlesque? Every mountain plant offers an equal interest to the artless botanist. For him the euphorbia is not celebrated or the borage ridiculous (besides which it has the most beautiful eyes in the world), and he fills his bag till it can hold not another blade of grass. Literary glory was invented for the use of children preparing their examinations. It matters little to the explorer of the mind of the past that this agreeable verse is by an unknown poet, or that profound thought by a despised thinker. A man and his work are so different in interest! The man is a physiological entity of value only in the environment that developed it. The work, whatever it may be, can keep an abstract power for centuries. This power should not be exaggerated or erected into a tyranny. A thought is very little more than a dry flower; but the man has perished and the flower still lies in the herbal. It is the witness to a life that has disappeared, the sign of an annihilated sensibility.

When, in the Gallery of Apollo, we gaze at those onyxes and those corundums in the form of conches and cups, those gold plaques engraved with flowers, and those flaming enamels, do we, before daring to rejoice, demand the name of the artist who created such objects? If we did, the question would be vain. The work lives and the name is dead. What matters the name?

"I, who have no wish for glory," wrote Flaubert. He spoke of posterity—of that future and, consequently, non-existent time, to which so many second-rate energies sacrifice the one reality, the present hour. Since none of Flaubert's books can serve as

---

15 *Recueil de quelques pièces nouvelles et galantes, tant en prose qu'en vers.* Cologne, 1667.

a pretext for moral teaching, he was well-advised. He did not wish for glory, and he will not have it, unless *Madame Bovary* retains during the next century its equivocal reputation and finds a place, in schoolboy-tradition, among the celebrated bad books. This is little likely, seeing that *Mademoiselle de Maupin* is already hard to read. But that which cannot be said for the future, either of him or of any writer of the last half of the century, may be said for the past. Gautier and Flaubert have known glory—the glory that they accorded themselves in the invincible consciousness of their genius. Glory is a sensation of life and of strength; a food-sprite would taste it in a tree trunk.

How amusing it is to listen to the eloquent professor who declares: "This book will not last." But no book lasts, and yet all books last. Do you know *Palemon, fable bocagère et pastorale,* by the Sieur Frénicle?[16] Well, this book has lasted, since I have just read it, and since I resurrect one of its verses, which is not ugly:

> O, que j'eus de plaisir à la voir toute nue!

It is time man learned at last to resign himself to annihilation, and even to enjoy that idea whose sweetness is incomparable. Writers might give the people the example, by resolutely abandoning their vainglorious hopes. They will leave a name which will grace the catalogues for several centuries, and works which will last as long as the matter upon which they are printed. This is a rare privilege, for which they ought to be willing to silence their complaints. And even were this illusory eternity to be denied them, as well as all present glory, why should that diminish their activity? It is to the passer-by, not to future humanity, that the wild cherry-tree offers its fruits; and even if no one passes, just as in the spring it has covered itself with snow, so it puts on its purple with the coming of

---

16 Paris, published by Jacques Dugast, aux Gants Couronnez, 1632.

summer. Life is a personal, immediate fact, which glides past the very moment it is perceived. It is bad reasoning to attach to this moment the age to come; for the present alone exists, and we must keep within the limits of logic in order to remain men. Let us be a little less primitive, not fancying that the next century will be the "double" of the present, and that our works will keep the position they hold today, or will have a worse. Our way of understanding *Bérénice* would afflict Racine, and Molière would gladly blow out the candles on nights when the *Misanthrope* is such a bore. Books have but one season. Trees, shrubs, or simple blades of grass, they die having sometimes sown their kind, and true glory for a writer would be to call forth a work whose shade would smother him. That would be true glory, because it would be a return to the noblest conditions of life. The witnesses of the past are never anything but paradoxes. They began to languish a few years, or even less, after their birth, and their old age drags on, sad and wrinkled, amid men who no longer either understand or love them. To desire immortality is to wish to live forever in the condition of Swift's "Struldbruggs."

"Such are the details imparted to me respecting the Immortals of this country...."—and man's sentiment continues to revolt against the idea of destruction, and the writer trembles at the idea of perennial obscurity. Our sensibility needs a tiny light in the far-off distance among the trees which line our horizon. That reassures the muscles, calms the pulses.

1900.

Success and the Idea of Beauty

I

In one of his *Paradoxes,* where he at times has a touch of Heine's irony or of Schopenhauer's wit, Max Nordau has sketched the Machiavellian plan of a school of success. The reverse of the usual morality would be taught there, and not virtue, but the art of arriving. This school already exists. It is life. Precocious eyes and ears take in its teachings from adolescence. There are young men who consecrate themselves to success, like others to the priesthood or to glory. Are they unreasonable? No. And contemptible? Why? Writing, singing, sculpturing are acts. Thinking, even in the silence of the night and in the depth of a dungeon, is an act. But what act is there that has not for its end its own accomplishment? The reasoner who has convinced himself will necessarily wish to persuade others; and the poet who admires himself, to force others to share his enthusiasm. Those who are contented with an intimate or restricted approbation are perhaps wise, but they will not be numbered among the strong. Though timid, though disdainful, the dreamer wishes the glory of dreaming, and he would dream with delight before throngs rapturously contemplating his eyes lost in an ocean of dreams and of nonsense. That would be success. Success has something precise which soothes and nourishes. It is a repast. It is a fact. It is the final goal.

Success is a fact in itself, and quite aside from the word or the act which it accompanies. The assassin who has accomplished his crime, step by step, experiences other joys than that of slaked avidity. He finds, in short, that success has declared for him; and, all pursuit thrown off his track, we understand very well the state of mind that Barbey d'Aurevilly has dared to describe. Yet crime, unless of a political order, is seldom publicly applauded in our civilizations, as among the Dyaks of Borneo, or the subjects of the Old Man of the Mountain. That is why, in spite of the celebrated irony, we shall not consider assassination "as one of the fine arts." It should at least be classed among the arts whose success is their one and only end, and which attach much less importance to their initial designation than to what they are called at the end. But that is not the subject of this essay, which is very serious, and whose words will all be carefully weighed. It will deal exclusively with works of art and, in particular, with literary works.

Success, then, is a fact; but, in the case of those acts which concern us here, it is a contingent fact and one that does not change the essence of the act itself. In this respect, I should be inclined to compare success to consciousness—a torch which, lighted within us, illumines our actions and our thoughts, but has no more influence on their nature than, when the moon is shining, the shadow of a passing train has on its speed. Consciousness determines no act. Success does not create a work, but sheds such light upon it that some trace of it almost always remains in the memory of men. A writer does not become Racine because he has been applauded before the footlights, and he remains Racine, even if *Phèdre* be played six nights in succession to empty boxes;[1] but he becomes Pradon, and that

---

[1] At the Hôtel de Bourgogne, while at Giénégaud his rival Pradon's play was received with great applause.

is a good deal. To be Pradon through the centuries is to live with a glory dark and disagreeable, sad and vain. Quite so, but it is scarcely less precarious than the life which we call real. Pradon is at once ridiculous and illustrious. It is impossible to tell the story of Racine's career without bringing his name into it. We search his works in order to understand that renown of a day which has been prolonged over so many morrows. It cannot be doubted; Pradon had almost no talent, though he was fairly adroit in his trade as a dramatic constructor. He was, as the journalists say, a man of the theatre. Critics have even gone so far as to claim[2] that, in order to have a perfect *Phèdre,* the play should have been written by Racine on Pradon's plan. That is absurd; but every success has its cause. The cabal explains nothing. The Duchesse de Bouillon would not have risked the battle on a worthless card. Pradon was known. His tragedy of *Pyrame et Thisbé* had been applauded. Ten years after *Phèdre,* and without any cabal, his *Régulus* was praised to the skies. He was therefore destined to enjoy a moderate reputation, such as *Solyman,* for example, brought its author, the Abbé Abeille, about the same date.

Was it fortunate for this commonplace poet to have encountered the Duchesse de Bouillon? Anticipating our modern methods, this terrible woman had hired the boxes of the two theatres, filling those at one and leaving the others empty. Today, she would have bought the newspapers in addition, but no one knows how much she paid the cackling of the newsmongers and the pamphleteers. It was a masterpiece in its way, since it succeeded marvellously; but what did Pradon gain by it? After much abuse, an ocean of posthumous blame. Not a day passes that some professor does not treat him as if he were a Damiens or a Ravaillac. Is immortality a sufficient reward for

---

[2] Bayle. And Racine, recognizing his adversary's craft, said: "The whole difference between me and Pradon is that I know how to write."

such treatment? Is shameful immortality preferable to oblivion? First of all, we should dismiss the shame, and ignore the abuse. Every success inflames the fire of hatred and deepens the descending smoke. That does not matter. Hate is an opinion. So is abuse; and so are the words that cast infamy. Success is a fact. The Duchesse de Bouillon could not change the essential value of the two Phèdres, any more than she could transmute "vile lead" into pure gold; but she could veil the gold and gild the lead, and she could force posterity to repeat her favourite's name. That was her work. It was well done and it has remained memorable. No one knew at the time which to admire of these two paintings with like frames. Pradon's friends were as powerful as Racine's. The latter had Boileau, the former Sanlecque, his sometimes successful rival. But Boileau's authority faded before that of Madame des Houlières, representing polite society and the *ruelles*. Thanks to the quarrel of the Sonnets, even wit ranged itself on Pradon's side, for the Duc de Nevers' still conserves today the most amusing malice. Molière, who detested Racine, and had already lent his theatre to a parody of *Andromaque,* would, no doubt, have favoured Pradon. His death spared the friends of sound letters that scandal. It was, therefore, a reasonable illusion around which success crystallized, and the witlings had no cause to blush for the part which they played. It is a pious lie on the part of the historians of French literature to pretend that the true public avenged Racine for the desert organized by Madame de Bouillon. The boxes of the Hôtel de Bourgogne had been hired for six days, while Racine's *Phèdre* had but seven performances. The public had understood. It obeyed success as dogs obey the sound of the whistle.

The reason is that success, though organized by fraudulent means, possesses a powerful attraction for the throng, even the literary throng. Assuredly, the theatrical public was, in 1677, far superior, in point of intelligence, education and taste, to the average public today. Yet it is seen applauding decidedly commonplace plays, while disdaining those of the first quality. The reason is that success, and especially theatrical success, can spring spontaneously from an accident,—from the agreeable face of an actress, from a fine gesture, from a well-timed bit of applause, from the caprice or emotion of a small group of spectators. The herd follows—since all men who come together are herds—and history numbers one more name and date.

The Americans—of the North, for in the South they have more finesse—never hesitate before success. What dramatic poem is it whose success has surpassed the enthusiasm aroused even by the *Cid* and by *Hernani? Cyrano de Bergerac.* Then this work is worthy of admiration, and they have it, as well as *l'Aiglon,* learned by heart in the schools where, though themselves illiterate, they cultivate learned wives. To repeat once more my real thought, I do not find that unreasonable. Let us not confound history, which is a complete or at least a consecutive novel, with the present, which appears to us in fragments, like a newspaper torn into a thousand pieces. How are these to be arranged, in what order? We have not the slightest idea. Our wisest and sanest contemporary judgment will be ridiculous in twenty years, because we lacked patience to reconstitute the entire sheet, or because the fire or the wind snatched away a number of the tiny squares. In this hazy state of our ideas, success gleams like an electric moon. Something undeniable is shining—something that the professors of philosophy call a criterium. But let us call it simply a fact, just as a flower is a fact, or a shower, or a conflagration. And what can be opposed to this fact, to contradict it? Almost nothing—the product of a judgment, certain men's notion of literary beauty. Moreover, this opposition is not radical, since beauty does not at all, in principle, exclude the chances of success. No bets should be placed on beauty. It would be imprudent to back her on even terms; but there are historic instances where the most beautiful work has also been the most warmly welcomed. In such cases success is adorable, like the sun which comes at just the right moment to ripen the crops, or the storm to fill the brooks and springs to overflowing. What is a beautiful book of which not a single copy remains known to us? What was an armless Venus before M. de Marcellus had summoned her from the abysses? Success is like daylight and, once again, if it does not create the work, it completes it by rending the shadowy veil by which it is encompassed.

There is another consideration which enhances still further the value of success, namely that, if the purpose of a work of art be to please, the greater will be the number of its conquests and the better this purpose will have been accomplished. Art has certainly a function, since it exists. It satisfies a need of our nature. To say that this need is, precisely, the artistic taste, is to say that a man likes coffee or tobacco because they satisfy his taste for coffee or tobacco. It is to say nothing at all—not even nonsense. It is to utter words without any meaning whatsoever. Things do not correspond with this simplicity in life—with this amiable relation of the kettle to its cover. Let us leave such explanations to the Christian philosophy of final causes. The purpose of art being to please, success is at least a first evidence in favour of the work. The idea of pleasing is very complex. We shall see later what it contains; but the word may serve us provisionally. Then this work pleases. A tower has suddenly arisen accompanied by the passionate plaudits of the crowd. That is the fact. This tower should be demolished. That is not easy, since by a singular magic almost all the battering-rams brought against it turn into buttresses which add their weight to the solidity of the monument. This monument must be convinced that it does not exist, this crowd that its admiration has not moved all those stones, that it lies; that it is hallucinated, or that it is imbecile. This cannot be done. It finds the tower beautiful. What can we answer, except "Yes, it is beautiful"?

The priest takes a wafer on the corporal and elevates it to divine dignity. He places it in the monstrance and shows it to the people, who during this ceremony kneel, bow, pray and believe. The work exalted by success is no less chosen by chance than the wafer by the priest's fingers; but its divinity, also, is no less certain the moment this choice has been made. The decrees of destiny must be respected, and popular piety not thwarted.

II

Yet, it is said, there is an aesthetic. There are several aesthetics, even. But we shall suppose there is but one, and that—always in principle—it has good reasons for opposing success, whatever it may be. Acceptance of an aesthetic obliges us to admit that there is an absolute beauty, and that works are deemed beautiful according to the degree of their resemblance to this vague and complaisant ideal. It is this aesthetic—admitting its existence for the moment—that is now to be laid open and submitted to the scalpel.

The sensibility which yields to success, or which produces it, is very interesting; but perhaps it will be permitted not to despise entirely, and at very first sight, the sensibility which opposes success and denies that the successful work is, as such, the beautiful work. These two sensibilities, though equally spontaneous, are not equally pure. The second is very mixed. The aesthetic which sums it up—an aesthetic as fragile as morality—is a mixture of beliefs, of traditions, of arguments, of habits, of conceptions. Respect enters into it—also fear and an obscure appetite for novelty. "On new thoughts let us make old verses." The new-old—that is what all aesthetics extol, for a caste must be flattered in keeping with its nerves and its erudition. The artist's judgment, in artistic matters, is an amalgam of sensations and superstitions. The simple-minded crowd has merely sensations. Its judgment is not aesthetic. It is not even a judgment. It is the naïve avowal of a pleasure. It follows necessarily from this that the aesthetic caste alone is qualified to judge the beauty of works, and to accord them this quality. The crowd creates success, the caste creates beauty. It is all the same, if you like, since there is a hierarchy neither in acts nor in sensations, and all is but movement. It is the same, but it is different. There, then, is one point established. In art, the opinion of the intelligence is opposed to the opinion of sensibility. Sensibility is concerned only with pleasure. If, to this pleasure, an intellectual element be added, we have aesthetics. The crowd can say: that pleases me, hence it is beautiful. It cannot say: that pleases me, yet it is not beautiful, or: that displeases me, yet it is beautiful. The crowd, as such, never lies; while aesthetic judgment is one of the most complicated forms of falsehood.[3]

It is very evident that absolute beauty exists no more than truth, justice, love. The beauty of the poets, the truth of the philosophers, the justice of the sociologists, the love of the theologians, are all so many abstractions which enter the realm of our senses—and very clumsily—only when blocked out by the sculptor's chisel. Like ideas conceived in the future or in the past, they express a certain harmony between our present sensations and the general state of our intelligence. This is especially felt in the case of truth, which is indeed a sensation uncontradicted by our intelligence; but any other intelligence may contradict it, or it may find itself contradicted by sensations of a different order or intensity.

The idea of beauty has an emotional origin, connected with

---

[3] In another essay, *Women and Language,* I have considered the lie as the mark of man as opposed to the animal. The superiority of a race, of a group of living beings, is in direct ratio to its power of falsehood—that is to say, reaction against reality. The lie is only the psychological form of the Vertebrate's reaction against its environment. Nietzsche, anticipating science, says: "The lie is a condition of life."

the idea of generation. The female who is to be the mother must conform to the racial type. That is, she must be beautiful.[4] Woman is less exacting, perhaps because man transmits very little of himself to his offspring. The first standard of beauty was, then, woman and, in general, the human body. Beauty, in the case of an animal, an object, is possession of something human in the form, in the character. A landscape can be described in terms almost all of which would apply to the beauty of a woman, and marble has her whiteness, sapphires are her eyes, coral is her lips. We have here a whole vocabulary of poetic commonplaces. To be sure, some of them should be corrected, and it should be noted that it is ebony which is black as black hair, and the swan which has a woman's neck. Beauty is so sexual that the only generally accepted works of art are those which show, quite simply, the human body in its nakedness. By his persistence in remaining purely sexual, the Greek sculptor has placed himself above all discussion for eternity. It is beautiful, because it is a beautiful human body, such as every man or every woman would like to unite with for the perpetuation of the race.

But another fact, more obscure, though not less certain, permits us to bring the idea of beauty back by another route to the very idea of sexuality. This is, that all human emotions, whatever their order, nature or intensity, awaken a more or less

---

[4] There is a presentiment of this in Montesquieu's remark, recently published; it is conformity that constitutes beauty *Æsthetics*. Father Buffier has defined beauty as the assembling of the commonest elements. When his definition is explained, it is excellent. Father Buffier says that beautiful eyes are those resembling the greatest number of other eyes; the same with the mouth, the nose, etc. It is not that there are not a great many more ugly noses than beautiful ones, but that the former are of many different sorts, and that each sort of ugly noses is much smaller in number than the beautiful sort. It is as if, in a crowd of a hundred men, there were ten dressed each in a different colour; it is the green that would predominate.

marked response in the genital nervous system. Sexual pathology has thrown light upon this. Perfumes, as well as the smell or sight of blood, noise and heat, intellectual or muscular effort, repose and fatigue, drunkenness and abstinence—the most contradictory sensations all favour the sexual impulse. Others, like fear, cold, vexation, also react upon a neighbouring and intricate centre in the genital system. Read the first chapter of *En Ménage,* in which M. Huysmans describes the effect produced upon a gentle, nervous being by the discovery of a lover in his wife's arms. Among the emotions which reverberate most surely on every somewhat sensitive organism, aesthetic emotions must be placed in the first rank. And thus they return to their origin. That which inclines to love seems beautiful. That which seems beautiful inclines to love. There is between the two an undeniable relation. A man loves a woman because she is beautiful, and he deems her beautiful because he loves her. It is the same with everything that permits associations of sexual ideas, and with every emotion which reacts upon the genital system.

But it is not at all necessary for a work of art to present a sensual picture in order to awaken ideas of love. It is enough for it to be beautiful, captivating. It stirs passion. Where shall we seek the seat of this passion? The brain is merely a centre of transmission. It is not a terminus. It is a happy and praiseworthy error to have made man's brain his absolute centre, but it is an error. The sole natural end of man is reproduction. If his activity had another goal, he would no longer be an animal, and we fall back into Christianity, to be confronted again by the soul, demerit and all the jargon employed by spiritualistic quacks. Emotion becomes conscious at the very moment of its passing, but it merely passes, leaving its image, and descends to the loins. This manner of speaking is perhaps figurative, and, moreover, I am not speaking of intense and strongly localized excitations. What is meant is merely that aesthetic emotion puts man in a state favourable to the reception of erotic emotion. This state is communicated to some by music, to others by painting, the drama. I have known a man—of a certain age, it is true—who could cheat a sexual desire by glancing at engravings. The reverse example would, doubtless, be less paradoxical. Aesthetic emotion is that from which man lets himself be most easily diverted by love, so easy, almost fatal, is the passage from one to the other. This intimate union between art and love is, moreover, the sole explanation of art. Without it—without this genital repercussion—it would never have been born; and, without it, it would not be perpetuated. Nothing is useless in deep-seated human habits. Everything which has lasted is, for that reason, necessary. Art is the accomplice of love. Take love away, and there is no longer art. Take art away, and love becomes merely a physiological need.

But it is less here art itself that is concerned than its emotional power, and there must therefore be grouped under the name of art everything in the nature of spectacle or sport—every diversion enjoyed in public, or with regard to which one communicates to himself his impressions. Fireworks can thrill quite as much as a tragedy. The sole hierarchy is that of intensity; but there is no doubt that the success of a work of art greatly increases its emotional power upon men in general. Hence, for the crowd, the quite natural belief that every successful work is beautiful, and that failure and scorn are always merited. In short, what the caste calls beauty, the people call success; but they have learned from the aristocrats this word truly devoid of meaning for them, and employ it to enhance the quality of their pleasures. That is not entirely illegitimate, success and beauty having a common origin in the emotions, their sole difference being the difference of the nervous systems in which they have evolved.

But very few men are capable of an original aesthetic emotion. Most of those who believe they experience it are like the people themselves, merely obeying the suggestion of a master, the bidding of their memories, the influence of their environment, the fashion. There is a passing beauty as precarious as popular success. A work of art extolled by the caste today will be despised by the caste tomorrow, and less trace of it will perhaps remain than of the work rejected by the caste and acclaimed by the people. For success is a fact whose importance increases with the dust it raises, with the number of the faithful come to accompany the cortège. The emotions of the caste and the emotions of the people are destined to the same end. Nature, which makes no leaps, makes no choice either. It is a question of making children. The sense of smell (or an analogous sense) is so highly developed in the emperor-moth, that a female egg of that rare butterfly attracts a throng of males to the spot where not one was seen before. This acuteness would be absurd if it merely served the emperor-moth to select a more delicate repast in the flowery flock or, in one way or another, to increase its pleasure and its spiritual advancement, the culture of its intelligence. It is an aid to the emperor-moth in making love. It is its aesthetic sense.

However, there are human natures, less diffuse or more refractory, in which the emotions do not react upon the centre of major sensibility, either because this centre is atrophied, or because the emotional current has encountered in its course an obstacle, a dyke, an impervious barrier. Let us, without examining too closely the aptness of the analogy, avail ourselves of the commonest and most striking comparisons. An electric current is thrown into a wire for the purpose of creating motion. The wire falls supported by a bit of wood and, instead of motion, heat is generated. The train which was to have been propelled burns. So the emotion, on its way towards the genital sense which it is meant to awaken, encounters a centre of resistance. It is broken, twists back upon itself, but becomes installed; and all the emotions of the same order, which pass by the same centre, will share the same fate. A wheel was to be turned, and we have fireworks. The species was to be preserved, and we have born the idea of beauty. Aesthetic emotion, even in its purest, most disinterested form, is, then, merely a deviation of the genital emotion. Aphrodite, who urged us to her cult, no longer troubles us. The woman has vanished. Noble forms are left, agreeable lines; but a horse also is beautiful, and a lion, and an ox. Fortunate short-circuit which has permitted us to reflect, to compare, to judge! The current hurled us on towards the sister of the goddess. Now it turns us from her, for she is less fair! It might be supposed that it is in the region of the intelligence the emotional current has become diffused, thus forming that mixture of emotion and intelligence which gives us the aesthetic sense. Intelligence is an accident. Genius is a catastrophe. We must carefully avoid even dreaming of a social state where health, equilibrium, equity, moderation, order would reign uniformly, where catastrophes would be impossible, and accidents very rare. Human intelligence is certainly the consequence of what we naïvely call evil. If the threads did not become cut and knotted, if emotion always attained its goal, men would be stronger and handsomer, and their houses would be as perfect as ant-hills. Only, the world would not exist.

III

Before returning to our point of departure, here is a résumé:

Two sorts of emotions share in the shaping of the aesthetic sense: emotions of a genesial nature, and all the other emotions whatsoever, in a proportion which varies infinitely with each man. The first are those which we feel when confronted with the perfect representation of our racial type. Apollo is beautiful, because he is the human male in all its purity. For the majority of men, every adventitious idea being rigorously excluded, the sight of the marble is agreeable because it evokes desire, either directly or, according to the sex, by counter-evocation. Stendhal's saying will be remembered: "Beauty is a promise of happiness." The sensualistic philosophy which enabled him to make this definition was not stupid. We shall be obliged to return to it, with science as a point of support. In short, it was then for the purpose of describing the "promise of happiness," that the word "beauty" was invented. And this word has been successively applied to everything that promised men the realization of one of their increasingly numerous and complex desires. Later, the emotional need having become extremely developed, it was also applied to all causes of emotion, even terrible or sanguinary; but these varied emotions, which make up the very life of man, have a goal—like the sense of smell in the emperor-moth. They penetrate us to make us remember that our one duty, as living creatures, is to conserve the species. Whatever sense they may have struck first, they recoil from it towards the centre of general sensibility. I think of those romantic lovers seen enveloped by the storm, possessing each other furiously, or of the gentle emotion of Tibullus, *quam juvat immites*.... The horrible, stupid, savage tragedies which delighted the Greeks and the French of the *ancien régime* were philters, and nothing more. If the great poets (like women, great poets have neither taste nor sense of disgust) had not taken the trouble to rethink the stories of Orestes, of Thyestes, of Polynices, we would deem these to be the delirious ravings of a society in its infancy or in its final decay. Not one of Racine's tragedies but has been played a hundred times in the criminal court by loathsome actors. You will find, if you look for them, in the special treatises of Ball and of Binet, and in popular works, examples of the transformation of any sensation whatsoever into sexual act. Here there are no categories, the field is unlimited. Men have been known for whom the smell of rotten apples gave strong and necessarily sexual emotions. Schiller always kept a stock in his table drawer;

but, as he possessed a refractory passage in which the emotional currents were in large part broken, he made verses, when he had inhaled them, instead of making love.

Here, then, we have a whole class of men in whom the emotions, arrested halfway, are transformed into intelligence, into aesthetic taste, into religious feeling, into morality, into cruelty, according to the environment and the circumstances, and according to an exceedingly obscure system of dynamics. It may even be said that this transformation of the emotions takes place, more or less, in all men. The emotions may chance also to react almost equally in all directions, a notable part travelling towards the genital centres while enough remains *en route* to produce a great philosopher, a great artist, a great criminal. Love seems peculiarly connected with cruelty, either by its absence or by its excess. The mimetic of cruelty is precisely that of sexual love. Duchenne of Boulogne has proved that by his experiments. In types of men like Torquemada or Robespierre, the emotions do not reach the genital sense. They encounter an obstacle which shunts them off towards another centre. Instead of being transformed into the need for reproduction, they are transformed into the need for destruction. But there is the Neronian type and there is the Sadie type, in which sexuality and cruelty become exasperated simultaneously and are intertangled. There are men capable of stronger emotional shocks than other men. Though divided and distributed towards two goals, the current remains strong enough to produce acts of great intensity. The same phenomenon, though in a less sinister form, appears when intellectual power comes into play simultaneously with genital power. Every man capable of emotion is capable of love, and at the same time, either of cruelty, of intellectuality, or of religious sentiment; but the emotional current is sometimes entirely absorbed by one of the human activities, and we have one variety of extreme types, the other variety being furnished by men of a great emotional receptivity and, consequently, of a great diversity of aptitudes.

But let us keep to the human average, and to the question of aesthetics. According to the quantity withdrawn from the emotional current, we shall, for example, have a spectator who retains from the tragedy its entire content of pure, robust beauty—who will go away in a state of intellectual emotion, less sensible to the murder than to the curve of the arm that struck the blow; to the curses and terrors, than the musical form which limits them, encloses them, gives them life. We shall also have a spectator who, in spite of a few glimmerings of intellectual emotion, leaves the theatre very much as he might a boxing-match or a bull-fight. There are the two extremes. One man, looking at a perfect statue, enjoys the grace of the curves, thinks: what a beautiful work! The other cries: what a beautiful woman! Between these two types there is a whole series of shading. For the man of average type, the idea of beauty scarcely exists. He will judge the work of art according to the intensity or the quality of his emotion. It gives him pleasure, or it leaves him cold, and that is all. It is this average type that determines success in art, the average type must be pleased. Its emotion must be stirred.

The representatives of the aesthetic caste also judge a work of art by the emotion it gives them, but this emotion is of a quite special order. It is the aesthetic emotion. For them those works alone that are capable of communicating the aesthetic thrill or emotion belong to art, to the category of beauty. Thus are excluded from art utilitarian, moralizing, social works possessing any purpose whatsoever outside this precise and exclusive goal, aesthetic emotion; also works of too sexual a type, whose appeal to genital exercise is over-direct, though they, too, respond—in their case with excessive clarity—to men's primitive notion of artistic beauty. In this way has been formed that aesthetic category which, eternally instable, ranging from realism to idealism (a certain idealism), from sentimentalism to brutality, from religious feeling to sensuality, remains, nevertheless, a closed garden.

Art is, then, that which gives a pure emotion,—that is to say, an emotion without vibrations beyond a limited group of cells. It is that which invites to neither virtue nor patriotism, nor debauch, nor peace, nor war, nor laughter, nor tears, nor anything other than art itself. Art is impassible, and as an old Italian poet said of love, *non piange, nè ride.* There is nothing about it either rational, or just, or consistent with any truth. It is a matter of the manners and customs of an intellectual caste. Born of an imperfection in the nervous system, the idea of beauty has picked up, on the way, all sorts of rules, prejudices, beliefs, habits, and it has constructed itself a canon whose form, without being absolute, fluctuates at any given moment between certain limits only. The restriction is necessary. All refined men of an epoch agree on the idea of beauty. Today, for example, there are certain touchstones: Verlaine, Mallarmé, Rodin, Monet, Nietzsche. To admit that you are not moved by the *Hands,* by *Hérodiade,* by *Eve,* by the *Cathédrales,* by *Zarathoustra,* is to admit that you are devoid of aesthetic sensibility. But works of quite another tone were formerly admired by the same human group. From Ronsard to Victor Hugo, the principle of beauty was sought in imitation. Artists imitated the classics, the Italians, the Spaniards, the English. In the last century, it was the effort after originality; and this produced even a few years ago an excess of false notes, but a music less flat, on the whole, than that which had so long wearied the Muses. Not that the artist imitated less, but he did so in the illusion of creating something new, and illusion is almost always productive. France is, moreover, the country where the idea of beauty has undergone the greatest number of variations, since it is peopled by an animated, eager race always attentive to what is happening and ready to make the acquaintance of everything strange and new, reserving the right to laugh at this novelty, if it does not suit their temperament.

Our aesthetic sense, then, has its caprices. But, historically variable, it is consistent enough at any given moment. There is an aesthetic caste today. There was always one, and the history of French literature is little more than the *catalogue raisonné* of the works successively chosen by this caste. Successes are shaped in the street. Glory issues from *cénacles*. As there are no examples to the contrary, this clearly must be admitted to be a fact—also this, that the *cénacles* become disgusted with the glories that escape them, and start running the streets. A fact is always legitimate, since it is always logical; but we can always oppose to it the repugnances of our own sensibility, or of a group of sensibilities. That is the way of the crowd when led by certain educated mediocrities, who make good lawyers, since they hate the house which they are fighting, and which does not recognize them. To the often obscure reputation established by the aesthetic group, we see, then, incessantly opposed the celebrities of success. It is easy to dupe the people by showing them, on the one hand, the poor solitary lamp; on the other, the harsh glare of globes and the mad riot of tulips.

But the people have little need of encouragement. They go quite naturally towards that which dazzles them. This also is a fact, and this also is legitimate. The public, led by cunning shepherds, does wrong to despise the confused gleam of the stars; but the aesthetic caste does wrong to laugh at the people's pleasures. It also does wrong when it monopolizes certain words and refuses to call works of art those compositions which, no less than those which they themselves admire, have as their aim to stir emotion. It is a question of quality, not of essence. The aesthetic caste suffers less from seeing a poor thing applauded, than a real work disdained. Its judgment, so sure in scenting false art, suddenly weakens, and is angered, because a votary of the popular taste does not incline before its admirations. It is always a mistake to appeal to justice; but it is madness to appeal to the justice of a social group. We should abandon all that; and shut ourselves up in an opinion as in a tower. It would be easier to cut the throats of a hundred fanatical admirers of *Quo Vadis?* than to convince them, and far less fatiguing. Literary justice is an absurdity. It supposes emotional parity among men belonging to different physiological categories. A work is beautiful for those whom it moves. Sensibility is incorruptible—popular sensibility as well as that of the *cénacles*. It is as incorruptible as taste and as smell. It was formerly imagined that there was such a thing as taste—an absolute taste worshipped in a temple. Nothing is more ridiculous, nothing more tyrannical. Let us leave men to seek their pleasure freely. Some want to have their feelings harrowed, others their spleen banished, still others their heart pierced. Different instruments are needed for each of these operations. Art is a form of surgery whose case is well equipped, and a pharmacopeia filled with vials of every form and odour.

People talk very seriously—that is, without laughing—of initiating the people to art. In less vague terms, corresponding to a certain scientific reality, this would mean so shaping the physiology of men in general, that emotion, instead of reaching the genital centre, spreads towards the aesthetic centre. The enterprise is not of the easiest. Poor people! How it is made game of, and how stupid, in their goodness of heart, are its intellectual masters! These really believe that taste for painting, for music, for poetry, is learned like orthography or geography! And suppose it could be, and suppose a few admirations had been imparted to a few workmen. What does it matter that the people do not admire what we admire? They would have the same right to ask us to share their enthusiasms. There is no absolute aesthetic. That which moves us is beautiful; but we can be moved only in the measure of our emotional receptivity, and according to the state of our nervous system. Insensibility to what we call beauty,—a very complex idea, the moment we leave the human form,—would seem, on the whole, to be merely the sign of a healthy organism, of a normal brain, in which the nervous currents go straight to their goal, without turning aside. But this simple state is rare. All men are capable of receiving certain aesthetic emotions, and all are eager for them; but almost no man is concerned with the quality of this emotion. The important thing is to be moved. No other monument since the cathedrals—perhaps since the pyramids—has so' stirred human sensibility as the Eiffel Tower. Confronted with all that junk reared on high, stupidity itself became lyric, fools meditated, wild asses dreamed. From those heights swept down, as it were, a storm of emotions. An attempt was made to divert it, but it was too late. Success had arrived. The more admiration a work receives, the more beautiful it becomes for the multitude. It becomes beautiful and almost alive. Emotional waves, starting from it, come, like combers, to break upon a people drunk and panting. The whole organism holds carnival. Stupid and beautiful, the genius of the species smiles in the shade.

Such is the social rôle of art. It is immense. There is an Australian bird which builds, as its nest, a big cabin where it spreads all the shining pebbles it finds. The male, amid the mosaic, dances a grave minuet before his troubled companion. This is art surprised at its obscure birth—at the very moment of its intimate association with the expansion of the genital instinct. A red pebble gives an emotion to a bird, and this emotion heightens its desire. Such is the social rôle of art. The people—and by the people, I here mean the mass of men—must admire. They must experience aesthetic emotions, must quiver with long nervous vibrations, must have rich and complicated loves; but, what matters it whence comes the cloud, so long as it rains!

I have merely wished to show the legitimacy of all aesthetic emotion, whatever its source, and of all success, whatever its quality; but I shall be readily believed if I confess that I retain my preferences for a certain form of art, for a certain expression of beauty. I depart in this respect from the common sentiment, that I do not believe it useful to generalize opinions, to teach admirations. To force admiration is almost as wicked as to force an entrance. It is for each man to procure himself the emotion he needs, and the morality which suits him. Apuleius's ass wanted to crop roses, because by so doing he would resume the human form. It is a very good idea to crop roses. It is one way to achieve freedom.

1901.

The Value of Education

Without being as widespread as it might be, and as it will be, education is very, much in vogue. We live less and less, and we learn more and more. Sensibility surrenders to intelligence. I have seen a man laughed at because he examined a dead leaf attentively and with pleasure. No one would have laughed to hear a string of botanical terms muttered with regard to it; but there are some men who, while not ignorant of the handbooks, believe that true science should be felt first as a pleasure. It is not the fashion. The fashion is to learn in books alone, and from the lips of those who recite books.

Cornelius Agrippa, who possessed all the learning of his time, and more, amused himself by writing a "Paradox on the uncertainty, vanity, and abuse of the sciences."[1] This might be rewritten today, but on another note. For a science does not have to be uncertain, vain and abusive in order to be useless to one who cultivates it; and, on the other hand, the certainty of a science, its interest and its legitimacy, do not confer upon it an absolute right to mental governance. We would even gladly agree as to the absurdity of a debate upon the certainty or uncertainty of the sciences. Some are aleatory, but the light-minded

---

[1] "A work," continues the translator, "which can profit the reader, and which brings marvellous contentment to those who frequent the courts of the *grands seigneurs,* and who wish to learn how to talk of an infinite number of things opposed to the common opinion." S. 1. 1603.

or interested alone call them so. The word science involves, by definition, the idea of objective truth, and we must abide by that, without further dispute, even conceding this objective truth, whatever repugnance may be felt for the indissoluble union of two words which then become ironical.

It is, moreover, a question not of science, but of education, for which science furnishes the matter or the pretext. What is the value of education? What sort of superiority can it confer upon an average intelligence? If education be sometimes a ballast, is it not more often a burden? Is it not also, and still more often, a sack of salt which melts upon the ass's shoulders in the first storms of life? And so on.

Education is of two sorts, according as it is useful or decorative. Even astrology can become a practical science, if the astrologer finds his daily bread in it; but what good can it do a magistrate to know geometry if not perhaps to warp his mind? Everything that concerns his trade—draughtsmanship and archaeology, even, and all notions of this order—will prove profitable to an intelligent carpenter; but of what use could an aesthetic theory be to him if not perhaps to hamper his activity? When it does not find some practical application or turn itself into cash, education is an ingot sleeping in a glass case. It is useless, not very interesting, and quite devoid of beauty.

There is much talk, in certain political circles, of integral education. This means, doubtless, that everybody should be taught everything—also, that a vague universal notion would be a great benefit, a great comfort for any intelligence whatsoever; but, in this reasoning, there is a confusion between matter and form. The intelligence, which has a general and common form, has also a particular form for each individual. Just as there are several memories, so there are several intelligences; and each of these intelligences, modified by its own physiology, determines the individual intellect. Far from its being a good thing to teach everybody everything, it seems clear that a given intelligence can, without danger to its very structure, receive only those kinds of notions which enter it without effort. If we were accustomed to attach to words only those relative meanings they admit of, integral education would signify the sort of education compatible with the unknown morphology of a brain. In the majority of cases the quantity of this education would amount to nothing, since most intelligences cannot be cultivated.

At least by the methods at present employed, which may be summed up in a single word—abstraction. It has come to be admitted in teaching circles that life can be known only as speech. Whether the subject be poetry or geography, the method is the same—a dissertation which sums up the subject and pretends to represent it. Education has at length become a methodical catalogue of words, and classification takes the place of knowledge.

The most active, intelligent man can acquire only a very small number of direct, precise notions. These are, however, the only ones of any real depth. Teaching gives nothing but education. Life gives knowledge. Education has at least this advantage, that it is generalized, sublimated knowledge and thus capable of containing, in small bulk, a great quantity of notions; but, in the majority of minds, this too condensed food remains inert and fails to ferment. What is called general culture is usually nothing but a collection of purely abstract mnemonic acquisitions which the intelligence is incapable of projecting upon the plane of reality. Without a very lively and universally active imagination, notions confided to the memory dry up in a dead soil. Water and sun are required to soften and ripen the sprouting seed.

It is better to know nothing than to know badly, or little, which is the same thing. But do we know what ignorance is? So many things have to be learned in order to appreciate and understand it! Those who might enjoy ignorance, since they possess it, are under too many illusions concerning themselves to find any frank refreshment in it; and those who would be glad to do so, have left their first innocence too far behind them. There have been moments of civilization when men knew everything. It was not much. Was it much less than all the science of to-day? This relativity may well make us reflect upon the value of education. It will aid us also to indicate its true character. Education is never other than relative. It ought, then, to be practical.

M. Barrès, in his last novel,[2] makes a deputy of Burdeau's type say: "Virtue, like patriotism, is a dangerous element to arouse in the masses." To these two abstractions should, perhaps, be added all the others, in order to decree a general ostracism against every idea that has not first been defined. And this would not mean the proscription of virtues or of patriotic sentiments, but simply this, that nothing is worse for the health of an average intelligence than playing with abstract words—than that false verbal science which is at once found inapplicable on entering real life. It is not a matter of being virtuous; how realize a word which is the synthesis of several contradictory ideals? It is a matter of accommodating one's nature to the vital conditions and moral traditions of his environment. It is not a matter of being patriotic. It is a matter of defending, against strange beasts, the purity of the spring where one drinks. It is not a matter of knowing the abstract principle in which the broad river of general ideas may find its source. It is a matter of making life at once an act of faith and an act of prudence. It is a matter first and foremost of preserving enough simplicity to breathe joyfully the social air, and enough suppleness to obey, without cowardice, the elementary laws of life.

Life is a series of sensations bound together by states of consciousness. Unless your organism is such that the abstract

---

2 *L'Appel au soldat.*

notion redescends towards the senses the moment it has been understood; unless the word Beauty gives you a visual sensation; unless handling ideas gives you a physical pleasure, almost like caressing a shoulder or a fabric, let ideas alone. When a miller has no grist, he shuts his sluices and sleeps, or goes and takes a walk. He never dreams of running his mill when it is empty, and wearing out his stones grinding air. Education is often nothing but the wind raised by the whirling of the bolts, and felt as words.

Teaching, from top to bottom—from the official to the popular universities, from the village school to the École Normale—is little else than a phrase-factory. The most valuable of all is the primary school, where one learns to read and write—acquisitions, not of a science, but of a new sense. If there were cut from the programme of the rest everything useless—everything inapplicable to life or to some profession or trade—scarcely enough would be left for eighteen months' schooling.

The greater part of the people still escape the tortures of listening to gentlemen who recite books. The children of the poor, freed from the scholastic prison, learn a trade, which is an enhancement of one's self, and begin to live at an age when their rich brothers still spend their time handling words which correspond to nothing real—tools which sculpture the eternal void.[3] This is about to be remedied, and here is the subject of a night lecture in a people's university: "The Development of the Idea of Justice in Antiquity." Even supposing—what is little likely—that the professor said nothing on this subject that could not be absorbed by a healthy intelligence, of what use could such

---

[3] Someone remarked in the course of a conversation: "The peasant is a real person; he is a scientist, a physicist." All modern political effort tends to turn the physicist into a metaphysician. This effort is well under way for the working-man, who begins to despise toil and value phrases. His surprise is great when he finds that the word has no effect upon reality.

a discourse possibly be to a popular audience, and what could such an audience derive from it applicable to its own humble existence? Less, assuredly, than from the old-fashioned sermons which were not afraid to flout its vices and to play upon its cowardice to keep it from low pleasures. But the clergy of the lay religion is grave and disdainful of facts. Souls speak to souls. The ideal descends upon the people. The first Christians at least met both to pray and to eat in fraternal union. After the repast, some arose to utter prophecies. The modern prophets live only on abstractions, and they gladly share this economical and ridiculous food with their brethren.

The man who has slowly acquired a science, has, aside from the social advantages which it offers him, conferred, by that very fact, a special force and agility upon his organs of attention. He possesses not only the desired science, but a whole hunting outfit in good condition, and all ready for new quarry. When he has carefully and patiently acquired a foreign language, he can afterwards, with far less effort, master the other languages of the same family. But, if he has had recourse to some time-saving method, the acquisition no longer possesses its proper value, and may even deteriorate more or less rapidly. Water, boiled very quickly, grows cold equally fast—a fact ignored by the manufacturer who had set up public boilers. By the time it had crossed the street, the water was as cold as if it had come from a cool spring. It is for this same reason that quick teaching by the lecture system is so particularly useless. The listener learns to believe and not to reason, which would still be a way of acting and of living.

Educational baggage is composed almost entirely of beliefs. Literature and science are taught like a catechism. Life is the school of prudent doubt. The school is a pretentious church. Every professor is equipped with an arsenal of aphorisms. The youth who refuses to let himself be made a target is despised. The inversion of logical values is carried to the point where certain intellectual acts—resistance to scientific faith, Cartesian reserve—are considered signs of unintelligence.

M. Jules de Gaultier has invented a new Manichaeism whose prudent employment will prove very useful in clearing up certain questions.[4] To the vital instinct he opposes the instinct of knowledge; but the former is not the good principle, any more than the latter is the bad principle. They have both their rôle in the work of civilization; for, if the latter develops in man the need to know at the expense of the forces which conserve his vital energy, it permits the intelligence, at the same time, the better to enjoy both itself and the life of the feelings. The spontaneous and unconscious genius of growing races refuses obedience to neither of these great instincts. Life does not exhaust its energy, which is immutable, but the modes of energy which it has assumed. We tire of feeling before we tire of knowing. This is what Leibnitz has naïvely expressed, and what has been repeated with him by all those whose intelligence is the vulture: "It is not necessary to live, but it is necessary to think." When this aphorism reaches the people, it means that the decadent vital instinct has begun to give up the struggle. The glorious flowering-time has arrived, but the plant will die once the insect horde has fertilized it and the wind has borne its seed to a virgin soil.

An ignorant mass forms a magnificent reserve of life in a people. Our civilization has failed to recognize this. It is an immense field of little flowers which exhausts the earth's vigour for the sake of a senseless effulgence.

Such ideas, even in the attenuated form of images, may seem barbarous to those who believe in the "benefits of education"; but it begins to be easier to find adjectives than arguments to regenerate this ancient and almost exhausted theme. Hearing so many journalists and deputies speak of education as a sovereign

---

4 *De Kant à Nietzsche.*

elixir, it is clear that they have tasted it at the sound, authentic source—that of the handbooks and the encyclopedias—but not from those detestable jars in which the evil genius of analysis slumbers. The true science, the "gay science," is singularly poisonous. It is quite as poisonous as it is salutary. It contains as many doubts as there are specks of gold in Danzig brandy. One never knows just where the intoxication produced by this heady liquor may lead an intelligence not too strong or too sceptical.

Compared with science, education is so slight a thing that it scarcely merits a name. What are elementary notions of chemistry worth, when we think of the chemist who handles bodies, composing and decomposing them, who counts the molecules and weighs the atoms? And what difference does it make whether a hundred thousand bachelors know the elements of the air? But already they know it no longer. Had they been taught to breathe, they would, perhaps, have escaped two or three diseases, a predisposition to which, or whose germs, they transmit joyfully to their children. It is necessary (despite a celebrated irony) to have a chemistry and chemical industries, but not to teach the man in the street the obscure principles of a vain science.

This is only an example, but it could be extended to almost all the elements of general culture. An average brain today resembles those experimental gardens in which flourish specimens of all the flora. Yet this garden has its special utility, whereas brains rich in little of everything are good for nothing. The ground has not even been turned into a parterre, but into a herbarium, and the dried plants are so commonplace, so defective, that they can be put to no decent use. The majority of the flower-beds, at least, should have been reserved for a profound and passionate culture. When this is done, the dead corners of the garden acquire once more a certain importance. They furnish manure and mould to warm the heart of the living garden.

We do not, then, pretend to say that general culture is useless.

It is indispensable as an auxiliary and a reserve, but as such only, and on condition that the general, superficial culture is accompanied by one or more sections of intensive culture. Alone, it has no value. If from the average level, we descend to the little gardens of the people, we now see, replacing rank but luxuriant grass, mere sickly growths already frozen by life. All the natural flora has been weeded out, and what was sown instead, in a soil poorly cleared and prepared, has been unable to come up because there was neither sun nor water. The sole interest of these ridiculous little kitchen-gardens is a tree, which is often tall and stately—some chestnut or linden. This is the trade in which the man has resolutely perfected himself. One of these trees alone is worth all the general cultures which have relegated it to a stony corner. It dominates them by its utility and by its beauty.

Man's justification in life is that he is a function. His days on earth must produce a result. That is why we shall eternally regret the abolishing of the trades by the extreme division of labour. Industrial civilization has withdrawn from a vast number of men the pleasure that they used to find in their work. A high salary may make a man satisfied to have worked, but it does not give him satisfaction in the work itself, the joy of employing the present hour in the realization of a definite object. Industry has operated against the artisan to the advantage of the idler, and also to the advantage of capital against labour. Any mechanical invention whatsoever has been more harmful to humanity than a century of war. The hedemonic value of muscular activity has been so far diminished that the only moments when workmen are conscious of living are those when the normal man relaxes—the moments of repose; and, necessarily, the temptation has been to dilate these hours of negative sensation to the point of absorbing in them the whole pleasure of living. Alcohol has afforded the means.

In order to suppress this source of excitation, people with

good intentions but unhealthy minds—that is to say, out of touch with reality—have contemplated opposing the pleasure of learning to the pleasure of drinking. If such a task were possible, physiological intoxication would be replaced by cerebral intoxication, and that would not be a very desirable result. To follow a day of muscular effort with an evening of intellectual effort, is to double the total fatigue without real profit to the man subjected to such a régime. Consider the poor wretch who, after ten hours of shoving a block of wood under the sharp teeth of a circular saw, comes back, after a picked-up supper, to listen to a gentleman address him on the holiness of justice! But justice would require the preacher to take turns with the artisan in shoving the blocks of wood and in comfortably studying the fruitful principles of social charlatanism. Poor people who, with their instinctive need of priests, believe themselves victors because, having denied a dogma, they now applaud the moral aspect of this same dogma, but deformed by hypocrisy and hatred! It is through education—a very ancient invention—that the clergy has dominated the people and the world; and it is through education also, that the lay preachers are determined to clip the last claws of the vital instinct.

For all these teachers teach desperately the negation of life. They infect the healthy section of the people with their own unhealthy habits of receiving sensation only by reflex, of watching in a glass the life they dare not encounter, and they do so with a certain good faith. The real object of this education is the implanting of a morality—a singular morality, whose precepts are almost entirely negative. By weakening the will to live, to the profit of an instable cerebrality, they fashion those enervated, obedient, docile generations which are the dream of second-rate tyrants. At the very moment when a race needs, merely to persist, all the forces of which its instinct is perhaps still the depository, they pour out for it, though in an impoverished, poisoned form, that very liquor with which the

Roman apostles tamed the surplus energy of the barbarians. If a rationalistic or religious protestantism were to pre-empt the sovereign place of our traditional, pagan Catholicism, we should share the fate of those conquered peoples.

But how is it possible not to be tempted to furnish rules of conduct along with rules of grammar? All we ask is that these precepts should not be depressants, but that the young should find in them, on the contrary, an incitement to activity—to all the activities. Education, in itself, is nothing. It can be judged only when its surroundings are examined by the light of this torch. A torch is useful, not because of its light, but because of the object on which its light falls. We see also an oven methodically heated with brushwood and faggots; but this heat is merely a sterile blaze if, when it dies down, the dough of the eternal bread be not given it to bake.

Education is a means, and not an end. It is painfully absurd to learn for learning's sake, to burn for the sake of burning. The very song of the birds is not in vain. During the periods of sexual calm the great love concerts are rehearsed. Considered as the precise instrument of a future work, education may have a very great, even absolute importance. It may be the necessary condition of certain intellectual achievements. It will be the staff of the intelligence; but, offered to a second-rate brain, directed simply and solely to the enlargement of the memory, it has no power to regenerate sick cells. It will rather serve to crush them. It will make them dull. It will divert from the natural needs of life the activities merely meant for daily exercise. Education ballasts unstable genius, giving it subjects for comparison and motives for reflection. To genius already established, it affords a little of that uneasiness which is the source of irony. It is sometimes a support for certitude, sometimes the cause of gravitation towards doubt. But it has an influence only upon intelligences in action or capable of action. It does not determine, it inclines. Above all, it does not create intelligence.

We are constantly offered examples of men who, educated in all that is taught, remain mediocrities, and who, though they have written for twenty years, have not even learned how to write. And, on the other hand, there are others who know but one trade, and who have read nothing but life. Their lucidity sometimes shames even genius.

1900.

Women and Language

Women's rôle in the work of civilization is so great that it would scarcely be an exaggeration to say that the edifice is reared on the shoulders of these frail caryatides. Women know things that have never been written or taught, and without which almost the whole equipment of our daily life would be rendered useless. In 1814, some Cossacks, who had discovered a supply of stockings, drew them on directly over their boots—a general example of our commonest acts, had not women, for centuries of centuries, been the patient teachers of childhood. This rôle is so natural that it seems humble. We are struck only by what is extraordinary. The powerful machinery of a woolen-mill overwhelms us. Who has ever felt moved at the sight of the simple play of a pair of knitting-needles? Yet, compared with these little sticks, the greatest power-loom becomes insignificant. It represents a particular civilization. The wooden or steel needles represent absolute civilization. In every field the essential should be distinguished from the accessory. In civilization women's part represents the essential.

It is easier to feel this than to prove it, for it is a question precisely of those acts which pass unperceived along life's path—of all sorts of things which are never mentioned, because they are not observed or because their importance is not understood. Thus physiology was long unknown, while curiosity was occupied with monsters. The continuous phenomenon ceases to exist for our senses. It was a city-dweller, or a prisoner, or a blind man suddenly restored to sight, who first noted natural beauty. There is an external physiology which disappears in habit. Analyzed, it reveals the most important voluntary act of our lives—voluntary, in the sense that they are contingent compared with the primordial movements of the life of a species; voluntary, if the will be regarded as the consciousness of an unconscious effort.

Whether sense or faculty, speech cannot logically be separated from hearing, but the education of the ear is much less perceptible than that of the vocal apparatus. They can thus be considered separately, or at least without observing a precise order in acquisitions which are entangled like all the activities of life. Moving, hearing, seeing, speaking—all these are connected. Imitation imposes itself upon all the functions at the same time, though an appreciable order of birth can be established for each of them. This order is of little moment in a study where it is question, not of the intelligence which receives, but of the intelligence which gives—of the exterior and not of the interior psychological life.

Speech is feminine. Poets and orators are feminine types. To speak is to do woman's work. Because woman speaks as a bird sings, she alone is capable of teaching the language. When the child attempts to imitate the sounds it has heard, the woman is there to watch him, to smile at him, and to encourage him. There is established a mute working contract between these two beings, and what patience the one who knows displays in guiding the one who tries! The first words pronounced by a child correspond in its mind to no object, to no sensation. The child, at this moment of its life, is a parrot, and nothing more. It imitates. It speaks because it hears others speaking. If the world were silent around it, speech would remain congealed in its brain. Thence the importance of a woman's prattle—an importance far greater than that of the most beautiful poems and of the profoundest philosophies. The function which makes man a man is the special work of the woman. A child reared by a very feminine and very talkative woman is formed rather for speech and, consequently, for psychologic consciousness. Left to the care of a taciturn man, the same child would develop very slowly—so slowly, perhaps, that it would never attain the full limits of its practical intelligence.

Were it possible to assign an origin to language, one would say that woman had created it; but the secret of all origins will forever escape us. Birds sing, the dog barks, man speaks. It is not easier to imagine a dumb man than a dumb dog or a dumb finch; and if these species formerly existed without a voice, it is not easy to see why they should have acquired an organ which many other animals, including the birds of the South Polar regions, get along very well without. If language were learned or acquired—if, in order to recover its first traces, the celebrated roots, it were enough to find the common mother of Latin and Sanskrit, of Greek and of Anglo-Saxon—it is not easy to see why the dog does not converse with his master otherwise than with his tail, his eyes and his yelping. But the dog will never speak, because the genius of an animal species is as rigorously determined as the forms of the crystalline species.

The view that the oldest language was composed of five or six hundred monosyllables, is now without value, though it had a certain force. It gave weight to several hypotheses whose absurdity was not at first evident. Yet nothing had ever been observed in any real language resembling an even unconscious reservoir of roots. Words are born of each other by derivation, coming into the world sometimes longer, sometimes shorter, than the original word. This derivation is always dominated by a real, living concrete sense. No man whose mind has not been spoiled by special studies, has the sense of roots. The ba, be, bi, bo, bu of the alphabets, are, according to the theory, so many roots; but a series of kindred meanings has not been attributed to each of these sounds. They are capable, even in the same language, of expressing them all, either by chance, or according to a logic whose laws are undeterminable.

The primitive element in speech is not the word but the phrase. Man's spoken phrase is instinctive, like the sung phrase of the bird, like the yelped phrase of the dog. The word is a product of analysis.

In order to give the word priority over the phrase, the older school started from this idea, namely, that the word is created after the thing has been perceived, man acting as a nomenclator, as a professor of botany who gives names to sprigs of moss. The reality is different. The child stammers words before knowing the objects of which these words are the signs. It is possible that man spoke—chattered—a long time before a fixed relation became established between things and the familiar sounds issuing from his mouth.

Thousands of languages can thus have been chattered successively on thousands of territories—languages lacking precision, essentially musical, a succession of phrases in which certain sounds only corresponded to realities; but these sounds, in spite of their importance, in spite of their utilitarian and representative value, may be supposed to have been at first almost as fugitive as the rest of the speech. An unwritten language never survives the generation which created it. Among savages each generation remakes its language so completely that the grandfather is a stranger among his own grandchildren.

If this primitive chattering be admitted, it will readily be admitted also that woman must have had a large share in it, while arousing the mind of the males by her laughter and her attention. Woman has little capacity for verbal innovation. Among so many excellent women writers, none has ever created a language in the sense of which this is said of Ronsard, of Montaigne, of Chateaubriand, or of Victor Hugo; but she repeats well—often better than a man—what was said before her. Born to conserve, she performs her rôle to perfection. Eternally, unwearyingly she rekindles from the failing torch a new torch identical with the old. It is in the hands of women—dancers in life's ballet, or melancholy vestals in deep caverns—that the *lampada vitai* shine. What woman has been historically, she will always be and she has always been, from before history even.

Certain words became fixed in the primitive chattering. This was the work of woman. Destined to attention by the monotony of her domestic labour,[1] she rebelled against the useless renewal of terms. Her life became complicated in those lands where the game was abundant, where nature was fertile. Men's needs increased with their wealth, and with them, woman's occupations. Having to work more, she had less time to listen to songs and speeches. Novelties succeeding each other too rapidly, upset her. She corrected the language of men who, in their turn, became disconcerted. Thus were born the words in common use, and thus the fixed sounds corresponding to realities in man's spoken song gradually grew in number.

Woman, whose memory is excellent, had also, from the earliest times, no doubt, retained the most musical, the most rhythmical parts of speech—some combination of phrases resembling those melopeias repeated insatiably by Negroes. Man created. Woman learned by heart. If a civilized country were one day to reach that state of mind in which every novelty is at once welcomed and substituted for traditional ideas and methods—if the past were to yield constantly to the future—then, after a period of frenzied curiosity, men would be observed falling into the apathy of the tourist who never glances twice at the same object. In order to recover their grip, they would be obliged to seek refuge in a purely animal existence, and civilization would perish. Such a fate seems to have

---

1 The idea of thus introducing attention into the world through woman is M. Ribot's, in his *Psychologie de l'attention*.

overtaken ancient peoples, so eager to renew their pleasures that their passing has left but hypothetical traces. Excess of activity, far more than torpor, has caused the decay of many Asiatic civilizations. Wherever woman has been unable to intervene and to oppose the influence of her passivity to the arrogance of the young males, the race has exhausted itself in fugitive essays. We can, then, be sure that, wherever a durable civilization has been organized, woman was its cornerstone.

Arising, as a reciter, before the creator, woman formed a repertory, a library, archives. The first song-book was woman's memory, and it is the same with the first collection of tales, the first bundle of documents.

However, the invention of writing came, like all progress, successively, to diminish woman's importance as archivist. Since everything that seemed worth remembering was fixed by signs on durable matter, it became woman's duty and pleasure to perpetuate what men condemned to oblivion. She has performed faithfully a task that matter has almost always betrayed; and so it is that tales which were never written, and which assuredly go back to the earliest ages, have come down to us. Women who had been entertained by them as children, entertained their own children with them in turn. In spite of the efforts of rational pedagogy, which would like to substitute the history of the French Revolution, or that of the founding of the German Empire, for *Tom Thumb,* mothers still put their good children to sleep with blue story or red, of love or of blood. But this oral literature, whose themes are so much more numerous than those of written literature, has been found to possess the greatest beauty, and consequently a supreme importance. We owe the salvaging of this treasure to woman's conservative genius.

She conserved also the songs, the tunes (and the dances accompanying them) which man sheds at the very moment when he leaves his youth. For him they are futilities, and he never gives them another thought. For woman, they are means of pleasing and she remembers them always. When hope has departed, she falls back upon them to live again the happy days of her youth. Thus do old women keep their hearts young.

Women do not seem to have had a great share in the invention of tales and of songs. They have preserved, which is a way of creating. Yet one finds, nevertheless, the mark of their mind in certain variants. Their tendency was to tone down the end of a tale, to quiet the effervescence of a song too rollicking. This invention saved the life of many of these small things, by making them available to children, whose memory is an exceedingly sure casket.

Along with literature women saved a whole collection of notions difficult to determine. It is not a question of the long string of superstitions, but of the element of practical science contained in these superstitions, these beliefs, these traditions. To estimate the importance of this chapter of human knowledge, one should make a sort of examination of his own consciousness. Then, after long reflection, he will be able to distinguish between things learned from books, and those which, while never written, everyone knows. What is truly indispensable for the conduct of life has been taught us by women—the petty rules of politeness, those acts which win us the cordiality or deference of others; those words which assure us a welcome; those attitudes which must be varied according to the character and the situation; all social strategy. It is listening to women that teaches us to speak to men, to worm our way into their will. For those alone who know how to please, can teach the art of pleasing.

Even before he speaks, a child knows the value of a smile. It is his first language, and nothing proves that it is absolutely instinctive. The animal has only those attitudes which are the sign of a need. Some are beautiful, some are pretty, but none are voluntary.

The smallest child's smile often veils an intention. Woman

has taught it the mystery of exchanges, and the fact that a friendly gesture can win food and other things essential to life. The little girl, better disposed than the boy to appreciate this teaching, knows the value of curving lips and of the wave of her rosy hand, long before knowledge of the vocal signs has permitted her tender brain the most elementary reasoning. It is, then, in her case, pure imitation; but the act is favoured by recollection of the end already obtained by the first attempt, and we have here a very curious and obscure example of an effect determining its cause in physiological unconsciousness.

Since women have little in their lives but passional relations, this very primitive play remains the basis of their social tactics. Men feel progressively the need of complicating this elementary science, but it always remains for them a supreme resource. To touch his conqueror, to please him—such is the last argument of the conquered.

All mimetic art is the work of women. Even when she is silent, a woman continues to speak—often with a sincerity which her words lack. Even when she is motionless she continues to speak, and she is often more eloquent then than with words or with gestures. The form of her body makes her breathing a language. The rhythm of her bosom betrays the state of her soul and the degree of her emotion. No speech finds a man more sensitive. But their eyes have at their disposal a keyboard still more extended, though less effective. With her eyes, with the varied curves of her mute mouth, woman can express her inmost thought. The eye pales or kindles, lifts or lowers its look, and it spells desire or disdain, anger or promise—so many pages understood by man the moment he has an interest in reading them. To these gleams and these movements, the play of the eyelids adds its value. This play is affirmative, negative, interrogative. It utters a short and decisive yes, or a yes of languor and abandon. It questions in the tone of anger or of complaining. It refuses with a half-abrupt closing of the pupil, which veils the eyes without closing them. But how many other shades there are, and how rich in speech the smile is, also! The whole woman speaks. She is language incarnate.

Her children will first be actors. Like their mother, they will learn how to speak at the start with everything that is silent—precious acquisition. Darwin found the first sketch of emotional expression in animals. There is an important element of instinct in the human mimetic. Woman has cultivated these primitive movements, has refined and multiplied them. To the signs of the true emotions have come to be added the signs of the false emotions, and then only has a language been created. Animal expression of the emotions is not a language, for it would be incapable of making believe. True language begins with the lie. There is a real meaning in the famous saying that language was given to man to disguise his thought. The lie, which is the sole external proof of psychological consciousness, is also the sole proof that signs are language, and not unconscious mimetic. The lie is the very basis of language and its absolute condition. Analysis of linguistic facts proves this clearly enough, since every word contains a metaphor, and since every metaphor is a transposition of reality, when it is not a wilful, premeditated falsehood. But, taking language such as it appears to us, and supposing each word to correspond to an object, it may be said that, if there existed a man who had never lied, that man never spoke. It is not, in fact, speaking, to say "I am afraid," or "I am cold," when you are afraid, or are cold. It is expressing an emotion or a sensation by means of verbal signs analogous to the trembling of the animal famished or frozen. But if, on the contrary, denying his emotion or his sensation, the man who is cold says "I am warm," and the man who is hungry says "I am not hungry," he speaks. Whether he employ words, gestures or written signs, it is by this, by the lie—that is to say, by consciousness—that the man is recognized. Lie, let it be understood, here signifies expression of an imaginary sensation. It is a matter of psychology, not of morality—separate domains.

If woman is language, she should be lie, and also consciousness. All three are connected and form but one. The first of these points has never been studied, but popular opinion favours it. Not only do women speak more readily than men, they employ a better syntax, a less haphazard vocabulary, their pronunciation is excellent. One feels that language is their element. The second point, the lie, is not disputed; but women are reproached with it, whereas it is the consequence of another gift and, moreover, an assertion of their spiritual nature. Women lie more than men. Then it is because they have a greater sentiment of independence, a livelier consciousness; and here we have reached the third point, without, it seems to me, a minute demonstration being necessary.

The hysterical lie has been spoken of. It is probable that there is an error here, not in the terms, but in the intention which has brought them together. If unconscious life is meant, it is an absurdity. The lie is, on the contrary, the very sign of consciousness, and there can be no lie save where there is full and active consciousness. A distempered sensation, expressed as felt, should not be confused with the intentional travestying of the exposition of a true sensation—the first term of the series with the last. The animal never lies. How could it? It is forced to express its sensation just as he feels it. If it wishes to bite, the dog curves his lips, shows his teeth. If you see it hold back, play the hypocrite, lie, it is because, through its contact with man, it has perhaps acquired a rudiment of consciousness—because its acquired education comes, at such a moment, into conflict with its instinct. Moreover, ruse—especially when applied to defence, or to the search for food—is something quite different from the lie. It is the acute form of prudence. The true lie is purposeless, without other utility than the assertion of a superior detachment. It presents itself as a negation of the ties that attach man to reality, in which respect it approaches poetry and art, of which it is one of the elements. Art is born, like the lie, of a lively consciousness of the sensations and emotions. It declares a state of extreme sensibility, together with a tendency to repel that reality whereby a man's senses were wounded. Art, whatever its form, implies a profound knowledge of the signs, and the will to transpose them, without reference to their customary concordances. The artist is he who lies superiorly—better than other men. If he lies with speech, he is the poet; with inarticulate sounds, the musician; with forms whose attitudes he fixes, the sculptor, and his art is merely the extreme development of the language of motion (of which the dancer represents a very fugitive stage); with lines and colours, the painter, and what does this last do if not restore to primitive hieroglyphics their true aspect and all their natural scope? Art is a language, and it is only that.

But if woman is language, how do women happen to have played so inconspicuous a part in the supreme activity of language? Critics, to flatter them, have alleged some sort of lateral heredity whereby it is demonstrated that, as the daughters of mothers less and less cultivated, going back through the centuries, it is not surprising that their aptitudes are inferior to those of the males. This is not to be taken seriously. For, if it be true that genius and talent are often directly related with anterior cultures, there are also sudden aptitudes developed by the environment. Why should not a girl find this aptitude in her flesh, like her brother? Moreover, for thousands of years now, women have been taught music. Yet it is perhaps the art in which they have least created. The cause lies deeper. Woman is language, but language is useful. Her rôle is not to create, but to conserve. She accomplishes this task marvellously. She creates neither poems nor statues, but she creates the creators of the poems and of the statues. She teaches them language, which is the condition of their science, the lie which is the condition of their art, the consciousness which gives them their genius.

When the child, about the age of six or seven, leaves the woman's hands, the man is already man. He speaks, and that is man in his entirety.

Woman's great intellectual task is teaching the language. The grammarians and their substitutes, school-teachers and professors, fancy that they are the masters of language, and that, without their intervention, men's language would perish in confusion and incoherence. They have been maintained for ages in this illusion, yet there is none more ridiculous. Women are the elementary, and poets the superior artisans of language, both unconscious of their function. The intervention of grammarians is almost always bad, unless it limit itself to a statement of the facts—unless it dare restore to the hands of women and of poets an influence which science could exert only with injustice. Here are some children who speak. They are going to school to have a lesson in grammar. They speak, and employ all the forms of the verb, all the shades of syntax, easily and correctly. They speak, but here now is the school, and the master succeeds in teaching them the nature of the imperfect subjunctive. For a function, the pedagogue has substituted a notion. He has replaced the act by consciousness of the act, the word by its definition. He teaches grammar. He does not teach language.

Language is a function. Grammar is the analysis of this function. It is as useless to know grammar in order to speak one's native tongue, as to know physiology in order to breathe with one's lungs, or to walk with one's legs. Compared with the rôle of the ignorant mother who plucks, like a flower, the first word blossoming on her child's lips, the teacher's rôle amounts to almost nothing. It is the mother herself who sowed this word which has just bloomed. For, if language be a function, it must be given the material on which to work. A woman's idle chatter, differing so slightly from that of the little girl talking to her doll, is the child's first lesson, and the one whose importance surpasses every other. Words are so many seeds which will sprout, grow and come to fruition in the young brain. Without this ceaseless random sowing, the child's linguistic function would remain inert, and only vague and perhaps inarticulate sounds would issue from its lips. It has sometimes been wondered what language children, brought up together beyond reach of the human voice, would speak. Perhaps they would speak none at all. It is a question that no one can solve. At all events, they would speak merely a rudimentary language—that is to say, one too rich, variable and entirely unknown. For innate roots exist no more than innate ideas. The child does not create his language. Still less does he secrete his language. He learns it. He speaks the way people speak about him in his cradle. He is a phonograph and at first functions no less mechanically. Before he is able to situate verbal signs with reference to the objects represented, he possesses them in great quantity, but in confusion, pell-mell. Later he will learn to utilize this wealth. Since he knows, on the one hand, the words and, on the other, the objects, the operation of combining them in his memory will be of the simplest, most natural order. The woman directs this combination joyfully, and she admires herself in her admiration of the child's progress. She believes that the double acquisition of the word and of the object is made exclusively at her command, and that fills her with pride. Thus, ignorance of the child's psychological mechanism assures the teacher's success.

Later, as poet, story-teller, philosopher, theologian or moralist—as creator of values, in Nietzsche's very forceful expression—the child will usually employ in her honour this language that he receives almost entirely from woman. The larger part of literature is the indirect work of woman, made for her, to please or to pique her, to exalt or to decry her, to touch her heart, to idealize or to curse her beauty and her love. The two sexes had to be thus profoundly dissimilar, foreign, opposite, for one to become the other's adorer. With equality of tastes, of needs, of desires, bodily differences would not have sufficed, nor the injunction of the species. Humanity could perpetuate itself without love;[2] but love would have been impossible without the radical divergences which render man and woman two mutually mysterious worlds. Only the unknown can be adored. There is no longer a religion where there is no longer mystery. In all societies, so long as she is young and beautiful, woman, even when a slave, is the mistress of civilization. The poets, inspired by her grace, heighten this supremacy by making her the theme of their songs; and poetry, which had, at first, no other aim than to tell the joys of possession or the pangs of desire, completed its evolution by creating love. For love, with all the sentiment, the passion, the dream, the happiness, the tears which this word implies, is at bottom a verbal creation and the imaginative achievement of the artists of language.

It is through poems, tales, traditional narratives, that ordinary man, inclined to enjoyment only, has learned to love, to enhance infinitely his commonplace joys and futile sorrows. Let us repeat here Nietzsche's saying—the poet has been the creator of sentimental values. But almost as soon as created, they have escaped him. Possessing herself of these new values, woman has turned them into instruments to assure her sovereignty. She has, in all simplicity, culled the fruits of language, her work.

How love has evolved under this domination, with all the benefits which have accrued from it, would be a long chapter in the history of civilization.

1901.

---

2 Copulation would have sufficed for that. Life in common, after fertilization, is extremely rare, except among primates and birds. Among carnivorous insects, the union is often mortal for the male whom the stronger female devours.

Note.—Philosophic deductions are of value only if they agree exactly with science; but then they have a value. I have therefore availed myself of the opportunity to complete the note on a previous page, concerning the lie considered as a vital reaction. Here is the scientific statement of the question:

"M. R. Quinton has been led, in the course of his investigations, to recognize that all living beings are divided into two great physiological groups, which correspond exactly to the two anatomical groups: *Invertebrates* and *Vertebrates*—The first, and lower group (Invertebrates), always in equilibrium with the environment, supporting all the exterior conditions, however unfavourable; the second, and higher (Vertebrates), not accepting these conditions, reacting against them, always in disequilibrium with the environment, maintaining internally the saline concentration of their origins, in opposition to the sea, which becomes more concentrated, or to fresh water which loses its salt; maintaining, moreover, its original temperature in opposition to a terrestrial environment which grows colder, *lying to the environment,* in short, in order to maintain its most favourable conditions of life. The lie, of which we speak, is only the psychological form of this reaction, on the part of the *Vertebrates,* against the hostility of the environment."

The obscure terms in this note (saline concentration, temperature of the origins) are explained in M. Quinton's book: *L'Eau de mer, milieu organique.*

Stéphane Mallarmé and the Idea of Decadence

> Decadence: A very convenient word for ignorant pedagogues; a vague word behind which our laziness and lack of curiosity concerning the law seek shelter.
> BAUDELAIRE: Letter to Jules Janin.

I

Abruptly, about 1885, the idea of decadence entered French literature. After serving to glorify or to ridicule a whole group of poets, it had perched, as it were, upon a single head. Stéphane Mallarmé was the prince of this ironical, almost injurious realm, as it would have been, had the word itself been rightly understood and employed. But, by an eccentricity which is a Latin trait, the academic world, in keeping with its normal but unwholesome horror when confronted with new tendencies, called thus the fever for originality which tormented a generation. M. Mallarmé, rendered responsible for the acts of rebellion which he had encouraged, appeared to the innocent ass-drivers who accompany but do not conduct the caravan a redoubtable Aladdin, assassin of the sound principles of universal imitation.

These are, after all, thoroughly literary habits. They have been flourishing now for nearly three centuries, and the most celebrated revolts have hardly lopped their branches—have never uprooted them. No sooner had the Romantic insolences subsided than the poet was forced to crawl, half-smothered, under the ancient greenwood which furnishes ferules.

These habits are also thoroughly Latin. The Romans, so long as they were Romans only, knew nothing of individualism. Their civilization offers the spectacle of a fine social animality. Emulation with them aimed at likeness, just as, with us, it aims at unlikeness. Once they possessed five or six poets—successful off-shoots of Hellenic grafting—they refused to admit any others, and it is quite possible that, their social, racial instinct dominating the instinct of freedom and individuality, no poet of fresh inspiration was born to them for four or five centuries. They had the emperor and they had Virgil, and they obeyed both equally until the Christian revolt and the barbarian invasion joined hands above the Capitol. Literary liberty, like all other liberties, is born of the union of consciousness and strength. The day when Saint Ambrose, writing his hymns, disregarded the Horatian principles should be memorable, for it marks unmistakably the birth of a new mentality.

Just as the political history of the Romans has furnished us with the conception of historical decadence, so the history of their literature has furnished us with the conception of literary decadence—the two faces of a single idea; for it has been easy to indicate the coincidence of the two movements, and to inculcate the belief that there was a necessary connection between the two. Montesquieu owes his fame to the fact that he was particularly the dupe of this illusion.

Savages find it very difficult to admit the possibility of natural death. For them, every death is a murder. They have not the slightest sense of law; they live in the domain of the accidental. It has been agreed to call this state of mind inferior, and it is inferior, though the notion of rigid law is just as false and as dangerous as its negation. The only absolutely necessary laws are natural laws, which can neither vary nor change. In the case of social and political evolution, not only are there no necessary laws, but there are no very general laws even. Either these so-called laws, confused with the facts which they explain, amount to nothing but wise and honourable assertions, or else they declare, though over-emphatically, the very principle of change. Empires, then, are born, grow and die. Social combinations are unstable. Human groups have, at different epochs, different powers of cohesion. New affinities appear and are propagated. Here there would be the material for a treatise on social mechanics, if the writer did not insist too rigorously on squaring his philosophy with the reality of unexpected catastrophes. For the unexpected must be left a place which is sometimes the throne whence irony flashes and laughs. The idea of decadence is, then, merely the idea of natural death. Historians admit no other. To explain the taking of Byzantium by the Turks, they make us listen to the murmur of theological quarrels, and the crack of the Blue's whip in the circus. Longchamps leads to Sedan, no doubt, but Epsom leads to Waterloo also. The long decadence of crumbling empires is one of the most singular illusions in history. If certain empires have died of sickness or of old age, the greater number, on the contrary, have succumbed to violent death, in the plenitude of their physical power, in the full force of their intellectual vigour.

Then, too, intelligence is personal, and no reasonable relation can be established between the power of a people and the genius of an individual. Neither Greek literature, nor the literatures of the Middle Ages, correspond to stable and powerful political institutions, Greek, Italian or French; and it is precisely now, when their material power has become negligible, that the Scandinavian kingdoms have decked themselves with original talents. It would, perhaps, be nearer the truth to say that political decadence is the condition most favourable for intellectual flowering. It is when a Gustavus Adolphus and a

Charles XII are no longer possible, that an Ibsen and a Björnson appear. In the same way, the fall of Napoleon seemed a signal for nature to clothe herself again joyously in green, and to put forth her most magnificent growths. Goethe was the contemporary of his country's ruin. In order to exercise and satisfy our tendencies towards historical scepticism, we should not, however, fail to oppose to these examples the phenomena of those doubly glorious epochs of which the pompous century of Louis XIV is the venerated model. After this, a few minutes' reflection will force us to adopt a somewhat different opinion from that which passes current persistently in text-books and in conversation.

Bossuet was the first to whom it occurred to judge universal history—or what he naïvely regarded as such—in accordance with the principles of Biblical Judaism. He saw the fall of all those empires upon which Jehovah had laid his heavy hand. This is the idea of decadence explained by that of punishment. Montesquieu's more complicated philosophy is perhaps even more puerile. It is impossible to name without a sort of disgust a historian who dates the decadence of Rome from the dawn of those admirable centuries of world-peace which, perhaps, constitute the one happy epoch of civilized humanity. The meaning of the words must be scrutinized closely. Then it will be perceived that they have no sense, and that memorable writers used them all their lives without understanding them. But however debatable, or at least however vague, it may be, the general idea of decadence is clear and distinct compared with the more restricted notion of literary decadence.

From Racine to Vigny, France produced no great poet. This is a fact. Such a period is certainly one of literary decadence; yet we should not go further than the fact itself, or attribute to it an absurd character of logic and necessity. Poetry was asleep in the eighteenth century, through lack of poets; but this failure is not the result of a too free flowering prior to that period.

It is what it is, and nothing more. If we call it decadence, we admit the existence of a sort of mysterious organism—a being, a woman—Poetry—who is born, brings forth, and dies, at almost regular intervals, after the manner of human beings. This is an agreeable conception—subject for a dissertation or lecture—but one which should be omitted from a discussion, which aims only at the anatomy of an idea.

The principal trait of eighteenth century poetry is its spirit of imitation. That century was Roman in its cultivation of this spirit. It imitated furiously, gracefully, tenderly, ironically, stupidly. It was "Chinese" as well as Roman. There were "models." The word was imperative. The poet was not obliged to describe the impression produced upon him by life; he had to watch Racine and scale the mountain. What a singular psychology! The same philosopher who sapped the idea of respect in politics, replastered and whitewashed it anew in literature. There were critics. While Goethe was writing *Werther*, they were comparing Gilbert and Boileau. It was a degradation. Must we seek a cause for it? That would be vain. To attempt to explain why no poet was born in France for a hundred years, with the exception of Delille[1] and of Chénier, would lead necessarily to explaining the birth of Ronsard, Théophile or Racine also. We know nothing about it, and nothing can be known. Stripped of its mysticism, its necessity, all its historical genealogy, the idea of literary decadence is reduced to a purely negative notion— to the simple idea of absence. This sounds so simple that one scarcely dares to express it; but, when superior intelligences are lacking at a given moment, the multiplication of mediocrities makes itself acutely and actively felt; and, as the mediocre man is an imitator, the epochs that have justly been called decadent are nothing but epochs of imitation. In the last analysis, the

---

1 It must be remembered that the Abbé Delille is not at all, as is commonly believed, a poet of the Empire. Almost all his poems and his glory date from the *Ancien Régime*.

idea of decadence is identical with the idea of imitation.

II

Yet, in the case of Mallarmé and of a literary group, the idea of decadence has been assimilated to its exact opposite—the idea of innovation. Such judgments have made a particular impression upon men of one generation because, doubtless, we ourselves were involved and foolishly flouted by "right-minded" critics; they were, however, merely the clumsy and decrepit modern version of those decrees with which the mandarins of every age have sought to curse and to crush the new serpents breaking their shell under the ironical eye of their old mother. Diabolical intelligence laughs at exorcisms, and the University has been no more able than the Church to disinfect it with its holy water. In the past a man rose up—buckler of the faith—against heresies and novelties. He was the Jesuit. Today it is too often the Professor who arises as champion of the rules. Here again we have the antinomy which surprises us in Voltaire and the Voltairian of yesterday. The same man, so courageous where justice or political liberty is concerned, recoils the moment it is a matter of literary novelty or liberty. When, reaching Tolstoy and Ibsen, he alludes to their glory, he adds (in a note): "Are these reputations—especially Ibsen's—firmly established? The question whether the author of *Ghosts* is a mystifier or a genius has not yet been settled."[2] Such, confronted with the unknown—with the not yet seen or read—is the attitude of a writer who, in the very volume here quoted, proves that he possesses praiseworthy independence of judgment. I need not add that, in his pages, the "decadents" are scouted on every occasion. How, after this, can we be surprised at the dull raillery of

---

2   P. Stapfer, *Des Réputations littéraires,* Paris, 1891.

lesser minds? A new way of stating the eternal truths is always a scandal for men—especially for men who are too well-educated. They feel a sort of fright, and to recover their assurance they have recourse to denial, to abuse, to derision. It is the natural attitude of the human animal in the presence of physical danger. But how have we come to regard as a peril every real innovation in art or in literature? Why, above all, is this assimilation one of the maladies peculiar to our time—perhaps the gravest of all, since it tends to restrict movement and to obstruct life?

For years Delacroix and Puvis de Chavannes, so different in their genius, were hooted and rejected by the juries. Under evidently contradictory pretexts, a single explanation is discovered—originality. The guardians of art feel themselves menaced by a work which reveals almost no trace of previous methods—one not visibly attached to something known and already understood. Each of them reacts to the provocation according to his own peculiar temperament. Formulae change, too, periodically. The eighteenth century considered non-imitation a breach of taste, and that was a serious matter at a time when Voltaire was erecting a temple, which was only a templet, to this sprightly god. For ten years, and up to a few weeks ago, artists and writers who refused to rifle the masters were branded decadents or symbolists. This last insult prevailed in the end, being verbally more obscure and consequently easier to handle; it contains, moreover, precisely the same abhorrent notion of non-imitation.

It was said long ago, considerably before M. Tarde had developed his theory of social philosophy, that "imitation rules the world of men, as abstraction that of things." This law is very evident in the particular domain of art and of literature. Literary history is, in sum, nothing but the chart of a succession of intellectual epidemics. Some have been brief. Fashion changes or continues in accordance with caprices impossible to foresee and difficult to determine. Shakespeare had no immediate influence. Honoré d'Urfé, during his life and after his death, was, for half a century, the master and inspirer of all romantic fiction. He would have reigned still longer, had it not been for *La Princesse de Clèves,* the clandestine work of a *grande dame.* The seventeenth century, part of whose literature was merely translation and imitation, was not, however, averse to moderate and prudent novelties. The reason is that, if it would have been discreditable not to imitate the ancients—or, strange as it may seem, the Spaniards, but only the Spaniards!—in their fables and phrases (Racine trembled because he had written *Bajazet),* it was a mark of honour to be able to give classic borrowings an air of freshness and novelty.

However, this literature itself very quickly became classic. There was thus a second source of imitation; and, since it was more accessible than the first, it soon came to be almost the sole spring sought by successive generations to drink and pray and water their ink. Boileau was deified before his death. As soon as he could read at all, Voltaire read Boileau. The principle of imitation was thenceforth supreme in French literature.

Leaving aside the exceptions—however memorable—this principle has remained very powerful and so well understood, with the spread of education, that a critic has only to invoke it, for a shamefaced reader to cast aside a new work which he has found refreshing. Thus the newspaper critics have kept Ibsen from being acclimatized in France. Thus, too, verse plays, imitative works par excellence, succeed even on the boulevards! These theatrical events, always much magnified by advertising, furnish excellent illustrations for a theory.

The idea of imitation has, then, become the very soul of art and of literature. It is no more possible today to conceive of a novel which is not a counterpart or sequel of a preceding novel, than it is to conceive of rhymeless verse, or verses whose syllables have not been scrupulously scanned. When such innovations nevertheless occurred, altering suddenly the accustomed aspect of the literary landscape, there was a flutter among the experts. To conceal their embarrassment, they began to laugh (third method). Then they uttered judgments. Since these productions in verse or in prose are not imitated after the latest models, or the works praised by the handbooks, they must necessarily spring from an abnormal source, since it is not familiar to us—but which? There were attempts at explanation by means of Pre-Raphaelitism, but they were not decisive; they were even a little ridiculous, so profound and invulnerable was the ignorance on every hand. But about this time appeared a book which suddenly enlightened all minds. A parallel imposed itself inexorably between the new poets and the obscure versifiers of the Roman decadence, praised by des Esseintes. The movement was unanimous, and the very ones thus decried accepted this opprobrious epithet as a distinction. Once the principle was admitted, there was no lack of comparisons. Since no one—not even des Esseintes himself, perhaps—had read the depreciated poets, it was no trick at all for any critic to compare Sidonius Apollinaris, of whom we knew nothing, with Stéphane Mallarmé, whom he did not understand. Neither Sidonius Apollinaris nor Mallarmé is a decadent, since both possess, in different degrees, their own originality; but for that very reason the word was justly applied to the poet of *L'Après-midi d'un Faune*, for it signified obscurely, in the minds of the very persons who employed it, something little known, difficult, rare, precious, unexpected, new.

If, on the contrary, it were desired to restore to the idea of literary decadence its real and really cruel meaning, it is not, we suspect, Mallarmé or Laforgue, or any symbolist still writing, who should be named today. The decadent of Latin literature is neither Ammianus Marcellinus, nor Saint Augustine, each of whom fashioned a language in his own manner, nor is it Saint Ambrose, who created the hymn, nor Prudentius, who developed a literary genre, the lyrical biography.[3] We are beginning to have a greater indulgence for Latin literature of the second period. Tired, perhaps, of ridiculing it without reading it, we have begun to glance at it a little. Before long, this simple notion will be admitted, that there is no inherent distinction between good Latin and bad Latin; that languages live and that their changes are not necessarily corruptions; that a man could have genius in the sixth century as well as in the second, in the eleventh as well as in the eighteenth; that classic prejudices constitute an obstacle to the development of literary history and to integral knowledge of the language itself. Had they been better understood, the poets in the library at Fontenay would not have served to christen a literary movement, unless the intention had been to compare idealistic with Christian innovators—a difficult and rather ridiculous undertaking.

III

I have wished here merely to attempt the historical (or anecdotal) analysis of an idea, and to indicate, by means of a somewhat elaborate example, how a word comes to have only the meaning which it is our interest to give it. Hence I do not believe it necessary to establish minutely the ground of Stéphane Mallarmé's claims to either hatred or ridicule.

Hatred is queen in the hierarchy of literary sentiments. Literature is, perhaps, with religion, the abstract passion which excites men most violently. True, we have not yet seen literary wars resembling the religious wars of—let us say—the past; but that is because literature has never yet descended suddenly to the people's level. By the time it reaches them, it has lost its

---

3 A genre which has degenerated into the complaint. But the complaint has had its great period. The oldest poem in the French language is a complaint and inspired, precisely, by one of the poems of Prudentius.

explosive force. It is far from the first night of *Hernani* to the sale of the play in illustrated editions. However, it is not hard to imagine a mobilization of German sentimentality against English humour or French irony. It is because peoples do not know each other that they hate each other so little. An alliance marked by close fraternization always ends in cannon shot.

The hatred which pursued Mallarmé was never very bitter, for men hate seriously, even in matters of literature, only when material interests come to envenom a little the strife for the ideal; but he offered no surface for envy, and he bore injustice and abuse as necessities inherent in the very nature of genius. It was only, then, the pure and unalloyed superiority of his intelligence that was derided, on the pretext that he was obscure. Artists, even when depreciated by instinctive cabals, receive orders, earn money. Poets have the resource of long articles in the reviews and in the newspapers. Certain of them, like Théophile Gautier, earned their living in this way. Baudelaire succeeded ill at it, Mallarmé worse still. It was, then, in his case, against the poet stripped of every social ornament that the sarcasm was directed.

There is, by accident, at the Louvre, in a ridiculous collection, a marvel, an Andromeda, carved in ivory by Cellini. It is a terror-stricken woman, all her flesh aquiver with fright at being bound. Where can she flee? It is also Mallarmé's poetry. The emblem is the more appropriate that, like the sculptor, the poet wrought nothing but cups, vases, caskets, statuettes. He is not colossal, he is perfect. His poetry does not present a great human treasure spread forth before the dazzled crowd. It does not express common, strong ideas, which easily galvanize popular attention dulled by toil. It is personal, shrinking like those flowers that fear the sun. It has no scent save at evening. It yields its thought only to the intimacy of another thought, trusty and sincere. Its excessive modesty, it is true, draws about itself too many veils; but there is much delicacy in this eagerness to flee the eyes and hands of popular appreciation. Flee, where could it flee? Mallarmé sought refuge in obscurity as in a cloister. He interposed the wall of a cell between himself and the understanding of others. He wished to live alone in his pride. But that was the Mallarmé of the last years, when, hurt, but not disheartened, he felt himself seized with the same disgust for vain phrases which had also, in the past, stricken Jean Racine—the years when he created a new syntax for his own use, when he used words according to a system of new and secret relations. Stéphane Mallarmé wrote relatively much, and the greater part of his work is stained by no obscurity; but, if later and towards the last, beginning with the *Prose pour des Esseintes,* there are doubtful phrases or irritating verses, it is only an inattentive and vulgar mind that dreads to undertake the delicious conquest.

There are too few obscure writers in French. So we accustom ourselves like cowards to love only writing that is easy and that will soon be elementary. Yet it is rare that books blindly clear are worth rereading. It is clearness that constitutes the prestige of classic literature and it is clearness that makes them so clearly tiresome. Clear minds are commonly those that see but one thing at a time. When the brain is rich in sensations and in ideas, there is a constant eddy, and the smooth surface is troubled at the moment of spouting. Let us, like M. Doudan, prefer marshes swarming with life, to a glass of clear water. One is thirsty at times, to be sure. Well, then, one filters. Literature which gives immediate pleasure to all men is necessarily of no value. It must first, falling from on high, leap in cascades from ledge to ledge, in order to flow at last through the valley, within reach of all men and of all stocks.

If, then, one undertook a definitive study of Stéphane Mallarmé, the question of obscurity would have to be treated exclusively from the psychological standpoint, for the reason that there is never absolute, literal obscurity in an honestly written work. A sensible interpretation is always possible. It will, perhaps, vary according to the evening hour, like the play of cloud-shadows on the velvet lawn; but the truth, here and everywhere, will be what our passing sentiment shall make it. Mallarmé's work is the most marvellous pretext for reveries yet offered men weary of so many heavy and useless affirmations. It may well be that a poetry full of doubts, of shifting shades, and of ambiguous perfumes, can alone please us henceforward; and, if the word decadence really summed up all these autumnal, twilight charms, we might welcome it, even making it one of the keys of the viol; but it is dead; the master is dead, the penultimate is dead.

1898.

On Style or Writing

I

> Et ideo confiteatur eorum stultitia, qui arte scientiaque immunes, de solo ingenio confidentes, ad summa summe canenda prorumpunt; a tanta praesuntuositate desistant, et si anseres naturali desidia sunt, nolint astripetam aquilam imitari.
>
> DANTE: De vulgari eloquio.

Depreciation of "writing"—that is, writing as an art—is a precaution taken from time to time by worthless writers. They believe it sound, but it is the sign of their mediocrity and the avowal of a secret regret. It is not without chagrin that the impotent man gives up the pretty woman whose limpid eyes invite him, and there must be bitterness in the disdain publicly proclaimed by one who confesses utter ignorance of his trade, or absence of the gift without which exercise of that trade is an imposture. Yet some of these poor creatures actually pride themselves upon their poverty. They declare that their ideas are rare enough not to need fine clothing; that the newest, richest imagery is merely the veil thrown by vanity over the emptiness of the thought; that what matters, after all, is the substance and not the form, the spirit and not the letter, the thing and not the word; and they can continue like this a long time, for they have at their command a whole flock of facile commonplaces which, however, fool nobody. We should pity the first group and despise the second, replying to neither, unless it be to say this: that there are two literatures, and that they belong to each other.

Two literatures. This is a prudent and provisional form of expression intended to divert the mob by according it a share in the landscape, a view of the garden which it may not enter. If there were not two literatures and two provinces, it would be necessary to cut at once the throats of nearly all French writers—a dirty job and one in which, for my part, I should blush to have a hand. Enough, then. The boundary is established. There are two sorts of writers: the writers who write and the writers who do not write—just as there are voiceless singers and singers with voices.

The disdain for style would seem to be one of the conquests of 1789. At least, prior to the democratic era, it had been taken for granted that the one way to treat writers who did not write was to ridicule them. From Pisistratus to Louis XVI, the civilized world was unanimous on this point—a writer must know how to write. This was the Greek view, and the Romans loved fine style to such a degree that they came to write very badly through wishing to write too well. Saint Ambrose esteemed eloquence so highly that he regarded it as one of the gifts of the Holy Spirit—*vox donum Spiritus*—and Saint Hilary of Poitiers, in chapter thirteen of his *Treatise on the Psalms,* does not hesitate to call bad style a sin. It cannot, then, be from Roman Christianity that we have derived our present indulgence for uncouth literature. Still, inasmuch as Christianity is necessarily responsible for all modern aggressions against external beauty, it might be supposed that the taste for bad style was one of those Protestant importations that befouled France in the eighteenth century—contempt for style and moral hypocrisy being

Anglican vices.[1]

However, if the eighteenth century wrote badly, it did so unconsciously. It thought that Voltaire wrote well, especially in verse, and reproached Ducis only with the barbarousness of his models. It had an ideal. It did not admit that philosophy might be an excuse for bad literature. It rhymed everything, from the treatises of Isaac Newton to garden manuals and 'cook-books. This lust for putting art and fine language where they did not belong, led to the adoption of a medium style calculated to elevate all vulgar subjects and to degrade all the others. With the best of intentions, the eighteenth century ended by writing as if it were the most refractory to art in the world's history. England and France signed, at that time, a literary pact destined to endure till the arrival of Chateaubriand, whose *Génie du Christianisme*[2] sounded its solemn dissolution. From the appearance of this book, which opens the century, there has been but one way for a writer to have talent, namely, to know how to write—no longer in the manner of La Harpe, but in accordance with the examples of an unconquered tradition as old as the first awakening of beauty in human intelligence.[3]

But the eighteenth century manner corresponded only too well to the natural tendencies of a democratic civilization.

---

1 On the importance and influence of Protestantism at this time, see the work of E. Hugues, pilfered by Protestant writers for the last twenty-five years: *Histoire de la Restauration du Protestantisme en France au XVIIIe siècle* (1872).

2 A book so little known and disfigured in its pious editions. Nothing could be less pious, however, or less edifying, after the first volume, than this curious and confused encyclopedia, where we find *René* and statistical tables, *Atala* and a catalogue of Greek painters. It is a universal history of civilization and a plan of social reconstruction.

3 In speaking of the eighteenth century, exception must always be made of the grandiose and solitary Buffon, in his tower at Montbard, who was, in the modern sense of these words, a scientist, a philosopher, and a poet.

Neither Chateaubriand nor Victor Hugo was able to abrogate the organic law which sends the herd plunging down to the green plain where there is grass, and where there will be nothing but dust, once it has passed. It was soon deemed useless to cultivate a landscape destined to popular devastations, so there sprang up a literature without style, just as there are highroads without grass, without shade, and without wayside springs.

II

Writing is a trade, and I should rather see it catalogued between cobbling and carpentry, than separated from the other manifestations of human activity. Thus set apart, it can be virtually denied existence under colour of according it special honour, and so far removed from every vital interest that it will die of its isolation. Given, however, its place in one of the symbolic niches along the great gallery, it suggests apprenticeship and the handling of tools. It repels impromptu vocations. It is severe and uninviting.

Writing is a trade, but style is not a science. "Style is the man," and that other formula, "Style is inviolable," offered by Hello, mean exactly the same thing, namely, that style is as personal as the colour of the eyes or the sound of the voice. One can learn to write; one cannot learn to have a style. A writer can dye his style, as he does his hair, but he must begin over again every morning, and have no distractions. It is so little possible to acquire a style, that one is often lost in the course of a lifetime. When the vital force diminishes, writing suffers. Practice, which improves other gifts, often spoils this one.

Writing is very different from painting or modelling. To write or to speak is to make use of a faculty necessarily common to all men—a primordial and unconscious faculty which cannot be analyzed without the complete anatomy of the intelligence.

That is why all treatises on the art of writing, whether they number ten pages or ten thousand, are but vain sketches. The question is so complex that it is hard to know where to attack' it. It has so many sharp points, and is such a thicket of thorns and thistles that, instead of plunging straight into it, one goes around, and that is wiser.

To write, as Flaubert and Goncourt understood it, is to exist, to be one's self. To have a style is to speak, in the midst of the common language, a peculiar dialect, unique and inimitable, yet so constituted as to be at once the language of all and the language of an individual. Style is self-evident. To study its mechanism is useless to the point where uselessness becomes a positive menace. That which can be recomposed from the products of stylistic distillation bears the same resemblance to the style distilled, that a perfumed paper rose bears to a real rose.

Whatever be the fundamental importance of a "written" work, possession of style enhances its value. It was Buffon's opinion that all the beauties found in a well-written book, "all the relations which constitute style, are so many truths quite as useful for the mind as those forming the substance of the subject, and perhaps even more precious." And, despite the common disdain, this is also the common opinion, since the books of the past which still live, live only by virtue of their style. Were the contrary possible, such a contemporary of Buffon as Boulanger, author of *L'Antiquité dévoilée,* would not be unknown today, for there was nothing mediocre about the man but his way of writing. And is it not because he almost always lacked style, that another contemporary, Diderot, has never enjoyed more than a few hours of reputation at a time, and that as soon as people stop talking about him, he is forgotten?

It is because of this incontestable preponderance of style that the invention of plots is of no great importance in literature. To write a good novel or a lasting drama, one must either select a subject so banal that it is absolutely nil, or invent one so new that genius alone can get anything out of it—*Romeo and Juliet,* or *Don Quixote.* Most of Shakespeare's tragedies are merely a succession of metaphors embroidered on the canvas of the first story that came to his hand. Shakespeare invented nothing but his lines and his phrases. His images being new, their novelty necessarily communicated life to the characters. If *Hamlet,* idea for idea, had been written by Christopher Marlowe, it would be merely an obscure, clumsy tragedy, cited as an interesting sketch. M. de Maupassant, who invented the majority of his themes, is a lesser story-teller than Boccaccio, who invented none of his. Besides, the invention of subjects is limited, though infinitely flexible. But, change the age, and you change the story. If M. Aicard had genius, he would not have translated Othello; he would have remade it, just as the youthful Racine remade the tragedies of Euripides'. If man did not have style as a means of achieving variety, everything would be said in the first hundred years of a literature. I am quite willing to admit that there are thirty-six situations for novels and dramas, but a more general theory can, as a matter of fact, recognize four only. Man, taken as the centre, may have relations with himself, with other men, with the other sex, with the infinite—God or Nature. A piece of literature falls necessarily into one of these four categories; but were there in the world one theme only, and that *Daphnis and Chloe,* it would suffice.

One of the excuses made by writers who do not know how to write, is the diversity of genres. They believe that one genre calls for style, and that another does not. A novel, they say, should not be written in the same tone as a poem. True; but absence of style means absence of tone also, and when a book lacks "writing," it lacks everything. It is invisible or, as we say, it passes unnoticed. And that is as it should be. After all, there is but one genre, poetry, and but one medium, verse; for beautiful prose must have a rhythm which will make us doubt whether it be merely prose. Buffon wrote nothing but poems, as did Bossuet and Chateaubriand and Flaubert. If the *Époques de la Nature* stirs the admiration of scientists and philosophers, it is none the less a sumptuous epic. M. Brunetière spoke with ingenious boldness of the evolution of the genres. He showed that Bossuet's prose is but one of the cuts in the great lyric forest where Victor Hugo later was a woodsman. But I prefer the idea that there are no genres, or that there is but one only. This, moreover, is in closer accord with the latest theories of science and philosophy. The idea of evolution is about to disappear before that of permanence, perpetuity.

Can one learn to write? Regarded as a question of style, this amounts to asking if, with application, M. Zola could have become Chateaubriand, or if M. Quesnay de Beaurepaire, had he taken pains, could have become Rabelais: if the man who imitates precious marbles by spraying pine panels with a sharp shake of his brush, could, properly guided, have painted the *Pauvre Pêcheur*, or if the stone-cutter, who chisels the depressing fronts of Parisian houses in the Corinthian manner, might not, perhaps, after twenty lessons, execute the *Porte d'Enfer* or the tomb of Philippe Pot?

Can one learn to write? If, on the other hand, the question be one of the elements of a trade, of what painters are taught in the academies, all that can indeed be learned. One can learn to write correctly, in the neutral manner, just as engravers used to work in the "black manner." One can learn to write badly—that is to say, properly, and so as to merit a prize for literary excellence. One may learn to write very well, which is another way of writing very ill. How melancholy they are, those books which are well-written—and nothing more!

III

M. Albalat has, then, published a manual entitled *The Art of Writing Taught in Twenty Lessons*. Had this work appeared at an earlier date, it would certainly have found a place in the library of M. Dumouchel, professor of literature, and he would have recommended it to his friends Bouvard and Pécuchet: "Then," as Flaubert tells us, "they sought to determine the precise constitution of style, and, thanks to the authors recommended by Dumouchel, they learned the secret of all the genres." However, the two old boys would have found M. Albalat's remarks somewhat subtle. They would have been shocked to learn that *Télémaque* is badly written and that Mérimée would gain by condensation. They would have rejected M. Albalat and set to work on their biography of the Duc d'Angoulême without him.

Such resistance does not surprise me. It springs, perhaps, from an obscure feeling that the unconscious writer laughs at principles, at the art of epithets, and at the artifice of the three graduated impulses. Had M. Albalat known that intellectual effort, and especially literary effort, is, in very large measure, independent of consciousness, he would have been less imprudent and hesitated to divide a writer's qualities into two classes: natural qualities and qualities that can be acquired. As if a quality—that is to say a manner of being and of feeling—were something external to be added like a colour or an odour. One becomes what he is—without wishing to even, and despite every effort to oppose it. The most enduring patience cannot turn a blind imagination into a visual imagination, and the work of a writer who sees the landscape, whose aspect he transposes into terms of literary art, is better, however awkward, than after it has been retouched by someone whose vision is void, or profoundly different. "But the master alone can give the salient stroke." I can see Pécuchet's discouragement at this. The master's stroke in artistic literature—even the salient stroke—is necessarily the very one on which stress should not have been laid. Otherwise the stroke emphasizes the detail to which it is customary to give prominence, and not that which had struck the unskilled but sincere inner eye of the apprentice. M. Albalat makes an abstraction of this almost always unconscious vision, and defines style as "the art of grasping the value of words and their interrelations." Talent, in his opinion, consists "not in making a dull, lifeless use of words, but in discovering the *nuances,* the images, the sensations, which result from their combinations."

Here we are, then, in the realm of pure verbalism—in the ideal region of signs. It is a question of manipulating these signs and arranging them in patterns that will give the illusion of representing the world of sensations. Thus reversed, the problem is insoluble. It may well happen, since all things are possible, that such combinations of words will evoke life—even a determinate life—but more often they will remain inert. The forest becomes petrified. A critique of style should begin with a critique of the inner vision, by an essay on the formation of images. There are, to be sure, two chapters on images in Albalat's book, but they come quite at the end. Thus the mechanism of language is there demonstrated in inverse order, since the first step is the image, the last the abstraction. A proper analysis of the natural stylistic process would begin with the sensation and end with the pure idea— so pure that it corresponded not only to nothing real, but to nothing imaginative either.

If there were an art of writing, it would be nothing more or less than the art of feeling, the art of seeing, the art of hearing, the art of using all the senses, whether directly or through the imagination; and the new, serious method of a theory of style would be an attempt to show how these two separate worlds—the world of sensations and the world of words—penetrate each other. There is a great mystery in this, since they lie infinitely far apart—that is to say, they are parallel. Perhaps we should see here the operation of a sort of wireless telegraphy. We note that the needles on the two dials act in unison, and that is all. But this mutual dependence is, in reality, far from being as complete and as clear as in a mechanical device. When all is said, the accords between words and sensations are very few and very imperfect. We have no sure means of expressing our thoughts, unless perhaps it be silence. How many circumstances there are in life, when the eyes, the hands, the mute mouth, are more eloquent than any words.[4]

IV

M. Albalat's analysis is, then, bad, because unscientific. Yet from it he has derived a practical method of which it may be said that, while incapable of forming an original writer—he is well aware of this himself—it might possibly attenuate, not the mediocrity, but the incoherence, of speeches and publications to which custom obliges us to lend some attention. Besides, even were this manual still more useless than I believe it to be, certain of its chapters would nevertheless retain their expository and documentary interest. The detail is excellent, as, for example, the pages where it is shown that the idea is bound up in the form, and that to change the form is to modify the idea. "It means nothing to say of a piece of writing that the substance is good, but the form is bad." These are sound principles, though the idea may subsist as a residue of sensation, independently of the words and, above all, of a choice of words. But ideas stripped bare, in the state of wandering larvae, have no interest whatever. It may even be true that such ideas belong

---

4 An attempt will be made some day in a study in the *World of Words,* to determine whether words have really a meaning—that is to say, a constant value.

to everybody. Perhaps all ideas are common property. But how differently one of them, wandering through the world, awaiting its evocator, will be revealed according to the word that summons it from the Shades. What would Bossuet's ideas be worth, despoiled of their purple? They are the ideas of any ordinary student of theology, and, uttered by him, such a farrago of stupid nonsense would shock and shame those who had listened to it intoxicated in the *Sermons* and *Oraisons*. And the impression will be similar if, having lent a charmed ear to Michelet's lyric paradoxes, we come across them again in the miserable mouthings of some senator, or in the depressing commentaries of the partisan press. This is the reason why the Latin poets, including the greatest of them all, Virgil, cease to exist when translated, all looking exactly alike in the painful and pompous uniformity of a normal student's rhetoric. If Virgil had written in the style of M. Pessonneaux, or of M. Benoist, he would be Benoist, he would be Pessonneaux, and the monks would have scrapped his parchments to substitute for his verses some good lease of a sure and lasting interest.

Apropos of these evident truths, M. Albalat refutes Zola's opinion that "it is the form which changes and passes the most quickly," and that "immortality is gained by presenting living creatures." So far as this second sentence can be interpreted at all, it would seem to mean that what is called life, in art, is independent of form. But perhaps this is even less clear? Perhaps it will seem to have no sense whatever. Hippolytus, too, at the gates of Troezen, was "without form and without colour" only he was dead. All that can be conceded to this theory is that, if a beautiful and original work of art survives its century and, what is more, the language in which it was written, it is no longer admired except as a matter of imitation, in obedience to the traditional injunction of the educators. Were the *Iliad* to be discovered today, beneath the ruins of Herculaneum, it would give us merely archaeological sensations. It would interest us in precisely the same degree as the *Chanson de Roland;* but a comparison of the two poems would then reveal more clearly than at present their correspondence to extremely different moments of civilization, since one is written entirely in images (somewhat stiff, it is true) while the other contains so few that they have been counted.

There is, moreover, no necessary relation between the merit of a work and its duration. Yet, when a book has survived, the authors of "analyses and extracts conforming to the requirements of the academic programme" know very well how to prove its "inimitable" perfection, and to resuscitate (for the brief time of a lecture) the mummy which will return once more to its linen bands. The idea of glory must not be confused with that of beauty. The former is entirely dependent upon the revolutions of fashion and of taste. The second is absolute to the extent of human sensations. The one is a matter of manners and customs; the other is firmly rooted in the law.

The form passes, it is true, but it is hard to see just how it could survive the matter which is its substance. If the beauty of a style becomes effaced or falls to dust, it is because the language has modified the aggregate of its molecules—words—as well as these molecules themselves, and because this internal activity has not taken place without swellings and disturbances. If Angelico's frescos have "passed," it is not that time has rendered them less beautiful, but that the humidity has swollen the cement where the painting has become caked and coated. Languages swell and flake like cement; or rather, they are like plane-trees, which can live only by constantly changing their bark, and which, early each spring, shed on the moss at their feet the names of lovers graven in their very flesh.

But what matters the future? What matters the approval of men who will not be what we should make them, were we demiurges? What is this glory enjoyed by man the moment he quits the realm of consciousness? It is time we learned to live in the present moment, to make the best of the passing hour, bad though it may be, and to leave to children this concern for the future, which is an intellectual weakness—though the naïveté of a man of genius. It is highly illogical to desire the immortality of works, when affirming and desiring the mortality of the soul. Dante's Virgil lived beyond life, his glory grown eternal. Of this dazzling conception there is left us but a little vain illusion, which we shall do well to extinguish entirely.

This does not mean, however, that we should not write for men as if we were writing for angels, and thus realize, according to our calling and our nature, the utmost of beauty, even though passing and perishable.

v

M. Albalat shows excellent judgment in suppressing the very amusing distinctions made by the old manuals between the florid style and the simple style, the sublime and the moderate. He deems justly that there are but two sorts of style: the commonplace and the original. Were it permitted to count the degrees from the mediocre to the bad, as well as from the passable to the perfect, the scale of shades and of colours would be long. It is so far from the *Légende de Saint-Julien l'Hospitalier* to a parliamentary discourse, that we really wonder if it is the same language in both cases—if there are not two French languages, and below them an infinite number of dialects almost entirely independent of one another. Speaking of the political style, M. Marty-Laveaux[5] thinks that the people, having remained faithful in its speech to the traditional diction, grasps this very imperfectly and in a general way only, as if it were a foreign language. He wrote this twenty-seven years ago, but the

---

5 *De l'Enseignement de notre langue.*

newspapers, more widely circulated at present, have scarcely modified popular habits. It is always safe to estimate in France that, out of every three persons, there is one who reads a bit of a paper now and then by chance, and another who never reads at all. At Paris the people have certain notions concerning style. They have a special predilection for violence and wit. This explains the popularity, rather literary than political, of a journalist like Rochefort, in whom the Parisians have for a long time found once more their ancient ideal of a witty and wordy cleaver of mountains.

Rochefort is, moreover, an original writer—one of those who should be cited among the first to show that the substance is nothing without the form. To be convinced of this, one has only to read a little further than his own article in the paper which he edits. Yet we are perhaps fooled by him. We have been, it appears, for fully half a century, by Mérimée, from whom M. Albalat quotes a page as a specimen of the hackneyed style. Going farther, he indulges in his favourite pastime; he corrects Mérimée and juxtaposes the two texts for our inspection. Here is a sample:[6]

Bien qu'elle ne fût pas insensible au plaisir *ou à la vanité d'inspirer un sentiment sérieux* à un homme aussi léger *que l'était Max dans son opinion,* elle n'avait jamais pensé que cette affection pût devenir *un jour* dangeureuse *pour son repos.*	Sensible au plaisir d'attirer sérieusement un homme aussi léger, elle n'avait jamais pensé que cette affection pût devenir dangeureuse.

It cannot, at least, be denied that the severe professor's style is economical, since it reduces the number of lines by nearly one-half. Subjected to this treatment, poor Mérimée, already far from fertile, would find himself the father of a few thin

---

6 M. Albalat has italicized everything he deems "banal or useless."

opuscules, symbolic thenceforth of his legendary dryness. Having become the Justin of all the Pompeius Troguses, Albalat places Lamartine himself upon the easel to tone down, for example, *la finesse de sa peau rougissante comme à quinze ans sous les regards,* to *sa fine peau de jeune fille rougissante.* What butchery! The words stricken out by M. Albalat are so far from being hackneyed that they would, on the contrary, correct and counteract the commonplaceness of the improved sentence. This surplusage conveys the exceedingly subtle observation of a man who has made a close study of women's faces—a man more tender than sensual, and touched by modesty rather than by carnal prestige. Good or bad, style cannot be corrected. Style is inviolable.

M. Albalat gives some very amusing lists of *clichés,* or hackneyed phrases; but this criticism, at times, lacks measure. I cannot accept as *clichés* "kindly warmth," "precocious perversity," "restrained emotion," "retreating forehead," "abundant hair," or even "bitter tears," for tears can be "bitter" and can be "sweet." It should be understood, also, that the expression which exists as a *cliché* in one style, can occur as a renewed image in another. "Restrained emotion" is no more ridiculous than "simulated emotion," while, as for "retreating forehead," this is a scientific and quite accurate expression, which one has only to be careful about employing in the proper place. It is the same with the others. If such locutions were banished, literature would become a kind of algebra and could no longer be understood without the aid of long analytical operations. If the objection to them is that they have been overworked, it would be necessary to forego all words in common use as well as those devoid of mystery. But that would be a delusion. The commonest words and most current expressions can surprise us. Finally, the true *cliché,* as I have previously explained, may be recognized by this, that, whereas the image which it conveys, already faded, is halfway on the road to abstraction, it is not yet sufficiently insignificant to pass unperceived and to take its place among the signs which owe whatever life they may possess to the will of the intelligence.[7] Very often, in the *cliché*, one of the words has kept a concrete sense, and what makes us smile is less its triteness than the coupling of a living word with one from which the life has vanished. This can be seen clearly in such formulas as: "in the bosom of the Academy," "devouring activity," "open his heart," "sadness was painted on his face," "break the monotony," "embrace principles." However, there are *clichés* in which all the words seem alive—*une rougeur colora ses joues;* others in which all seem dead—*il était au comble des ses vœux*. But this last was formed at a time when the word *comble* was thoroughly alive and quite concrete. It is because it still contains the residue of a sensible image that its union with *vœux* displeases us. In the preceding example the word colorer has become abstract, since the concrete verb expressing this idea is *colorier*, and goes badly with *rougeur* and *joues*. I do not know just where a minute work on this part of the language, in which the fermentation is still unfinished, would lead us; but no doubt in the end it would be quite easy to demonstrate that, in the true notion of the *cliché*, incoherence has its place by the side of triteness. There would be matter in such a study for reasoned opinions that M. Albalat might render fruitful for the practice of style.

VI

It is to be regretted that he has dismissed the subject of periphrasis in a few lines. We expected an analysis of this curious tendency to replace by a description the word which is the sign of the thing in question. This malady, which is very ancient,

---

7 See the chapter on the *cliché*, in my book, *L'Esthétique de la Langue française*.

since enigmas have been found on Babylonian cylinders (that of the wind very nearly in the terms employed by our children), is perhaps the very origin of all poetry. If the secret of being a bore consists of saying everything, the secret of pleasing lies in saying just enough to be, not understood even, but divined. Periphrasis, as handled by the didactic poets, is perhaps ridiculous only because of the lack of poetic power which it indicates; for there are many agreeable ways of not naming what it is desired to suggest. The true poet, master of his speech, employs only periphrases at once so new and so clear in their shadowy half-light, that any slightly sensual intelligence prefers them to the too absolute word. He wishes neither to describe, to pique the curiosity, nor to show off his learning; but, whatever he does, he employs periphrases, and it is by no means certain that all those he creates will remain fresh long. The periphrasis is a metaphor, and thus has the same life-span as a metaphor. It is far indeed from the vague and purely musical periphrases of Verlaine:

> *Parfois aussi le dard d'un insecte jaloux*
> *Inquiétait le col des belles sous les branches,*

to the mythological enigmas of a Lebrun, who calls the silkworm

> *"L'amant des feuilles de Thisbé."*

Here M. Albalat appropriately quotes Buffon to the effect that nothing does more to degrade a writer than the pains he takes to "express common or ordinary things in an eccentric or pompous manner. We pity him for having spent so much time making new combinations of syllables only to say what is said by everybody." Delille won fame by his fondness for the didactic periphrasis, but I think he has been misjudged. It is not fear of the right word that makes him describe what he should have named, but rather his rigid system of poetics, and his mediocre talent. He lacks precision because he lacks power, and he is very bad only when he is not precise. But whether as a result of method or emasculation, we are indebted to him for some amusing enigmas:

> *Ces monstres qui de loin semblent un vaste écueil.*
>
> *L'animal recouvert de son épaisse croûte,*
> *Celui dont la coquille est arrondie en voûte.*
>
> *L'équivoque habitant de la terre et des ondes.*
>
> *Et cet oiseau parleur que sa triste beauté*
> *Ne dédommage pas de sa stérilité.*

It should not, however, be thought that the *Homme des Champs,* from which these charades are taken, is a poem entirely to be despised. The Abbé Delille had his merits and, once our ears, deprived of the pleasures of rhythm and of number, have become exhausted by the new versification, we may recover a certain charm in full and sonorous verses which are by no means tiresome, and in landscapes which, while somewhat severe, are broad and full of air.

> *... Soit qu'une fraîche aurore*
> *Donne la vie aux fleurs qui s'empressent d'éclore,*
> *Soit que l'astre du monde, en achevant son tour,*
> *Jette languissamment les restes d'un beau jour.*

VII

Yet M. Albalat asks how it is possible to be personal and original. His answer is not very clear. He counsels hard work and concludes that originality implies an incessant effort. This is a very regrettable illusion. Secondary qualities would, doubtless, be easier to acquire, but is concision, for example, an absolute quality? Are Rabelais and Victor Hugo, who were great accumulators of words, to be blamed because M. de Pontmartin was also in the habit of stringing together all the words that came into his head, and of heaping up as many as a dozen or fifteen epithets in a single sentence? The examples given by Albalat are very amusing; but if Gargantua had not played as many as two hundred and sixteen different and agreeable games under the eye of Ponocrates, we should feel very sorry, though "the great rules of the game are eternal."

Concision is sometimes the merit of dull imaginations. Harmony is a rarer and more decisive quality. There is no comment to be made on what Albalat says in this connection, unless it be that he believes a trifle too much in the necessary relations between the lightness or heaviness of a word, for example, and the idea which it expresses. This is an illusion which springs from our habits of thought, and an analysis of the sounds destroys it completely. It is not merely, says Villemain, imitation of the Greek or the Latin *fremere* that has given us the word *frémir;* it is also the relation of its sound to the emotion expressed. *Horreur, terreur, doux, suave, rugir, soupirer, pesant, léger,* come to us not only from Latin, but from an intimate sense which has recognized and adopted them as analogous to the impression produced by the object.[8] If Villemain, whose opinion M. Albalat accepted, had been better versed in linguistics, he would doubtless have invoked the theory of roots, which at one time gave to his nonsense an appearance of scientific force. As it stands, the celebrated orator's brief paragraph would afford very agreeable matter for discussion. It is quite evident that if *suave* and *suaire* invoke impressions generally remote from each other, this is not because of the quality of their sound. In English, *sweet* and *sweat* are words which resemble each

---

8 *L'Art d'écrire,* p. 138.

other. *Doux* is not more *doux* than *toux* and the other monosyllables of the same tone. Is *rugir* more violent than *rougir* or *vagir*? *Léger* is the contraction of a Latin word of five syllables, *leviarium*. If *légère* carries with it its own meaning, does *mégère* likewise? *Pesant* is neither more nor less heavy than *pensant*, the two forms being, moreover, doublets of a single Latin original, *pensare*. As for *lourd*, this is *luridus*, which meant many things: yellow, wild, savage, strange, peasant, heavy—such, doubtless, is its genealogy. *Lourd* is no more heavy than *fauve* is cruel. Think also of *mauve* and *velours*. If the English *thin* means the same as the French *mince*, how does it happen that the idea of its opposite, *épais*, is expressed by *thick*? Words are negative sounds which the mind charges with whatever sense it pleases. There are coincidences, chance agreements, between certain sounds and certain ideas. There are *frémir, frayeur, froid, frileux, frisson*. Yes; but there are also: *frein, frère, frêle, frêne, fret, frime*, and twenty other analogous sonorities, each of which is provided with a very different meaning.

M. Albalat is more successful in the balance of the two chapters where he treats successively word harmony and sentence harmony. He is right in calling the Goncourts' style *un style désécrit*. This is still more strikingly true applied to Loti, in whose work there are no longer any sentences. His pages are thickets of phrases. The tree has been felled, its branches have been lopped; there is nothing left but to make faggots of them.

Beginning with the ninth lesson, *L'Art d'écrire* becomes still more didactic, and we encounter Invention, Disposition and Elocution. I should find it hard to explain just how M. Albalat succeeds in separating these three phases of composition, which are really one. The *art of developing a subject* has been refused me by Providence. I leave all that to the unconscious, nor do I know anything more of the *art of invention*. I believe that an author invents by reversing the method of Newton—that is, without ever thinking about it, while, as for elocution,

I should hesitate to trust myself to the method of recasting. One does not recast, one remakes, and it is so tedious to do the same thing twice, that I approve of those who throw the stone at the first turn of the sling. But here is what proves the inanity of literary counsels: Théophile Gautier wrote the complicated pages of *Capitaine Fracasse* at odd moments on a printer's table, among half-opened bundles of papers, in the stench of oil and ink, and it is said that Buffon recopied eighteen times the *Époques de la Nature*.[9] This divergence is of no importance, since, as M. Albalat should have said, there are writers who make their corrections mentally, putting on paper only the swift or sluggish product of the unconscious, while there are others who need to see exteriorized what they have written, and to see it more than once, in order to correct it—that is, to understand it. Yet, even in the case of mental corrections, exterior revision is often profitable, provided, as Condillac puts it, the writer knows how to stop, to bring to a conclusion.[10] But too often the demon of Betterment has tormented and sterilized intelligence. It is also true that it is a great misfortune to lack self-criticism. Who will dare to choose between the writer who does not know what he is doing, and the one who, endowed with a double nature, can watch himself as he works? There is Verlaine and there is Mallarmé. One must follow the bent of one's own genius.

M. Albalat excels in definitions. "Description is the animated depiction of objects." He means that, in order to describe, a writer must, like a painter, place himself before the landscape, whether this be real or imaginary. Judging by the analysis that he makes of a page of *Télémaque,* it seems clear that Fénelon was only moderately endowed with visual imagination, and more

---

9 Or rather, had them copied by his secretaries. He afterwards reworked the clean copy. There is a whole volume on this subject: *Les Manuscrits de Buffon,* by P. Flourens, Paris, Garnier, 1860.
10 There is, on this point, a pretty passage from Quintilian, quoted by M. Albalat, p. 213.

moderately still with the gift of words. In the first twenty lines of the description of Calypso's grotto, the word *doux* occurs three times, and the verb *former* four. This has, indeed, become for us the very type of the inexpressive style, but I persist in believing that it once had its freshness and grace, and that the appeal which it made when it appeared was not unjustified. We smile at this opulence of gilt paper and painted flowers—the ideal of an archbishop who had remained a theological student—and forget that no one had described nature since *Astrée*. Those sweet oranges, those syrups diluted with spring-water, were refreshments fit for Paradise. It would be cruel to compare Fénelon, not with Homer, but even with the Homer of Leconte de Lisle. Translations too well done—those that may be said to possess literary literalness—have in fact the inevitable result of transforming into concrete, living images everything which had become abstract in the original. Did λευκοβραχίων mean one who had white arms, or was it merely a worn-out epithet? Did λευκάκανθα suggest an image such as *blanche épine,* or a neutral idea like aubépine, which has lost its representative value? We cannot tell; but, judging dead languages by the living, we must suppose that most of the Homeric epithets had already reached the stage of abstraction in Homer's own time.[11] It is possible that foreigners may find in a work as outworn for us as *Télémaque,* the same pleasure which we derive from the *Iliad* done in bas-relief by Leconte de Lisle. *Mille fleurs naissantes émaillaient les tapis verts* is a *cliché* only when read for the hundredth time. New, the image would be ingenious and pictorial. Poe's poems, translated by Mallarmé, acquired a life at once mysterious and precise which they do not possess to the same degree in the original, and, from Tennyson's Mariana, agreeable verse

---

11 I take it for granted that the reader no longer believes that the Homeric poems were composed at haphazard by a multitude of rhapsodists of genius, and that it was enough to string these improvisations together to get the *Iliad* and the *Odyssey*.

full of commonplaces and padding, grey in tone, the same poet, by substituting the concrete for the abstract, made a fresco of lovely autumnal colouring. I offer these remarks merely as a preface to a theory of translation. They will suffice here to indicate that, where it is a question of style, comparison should be made only between texts in the same language and belonging to the same period.

It is very difficult, after fifty years, to appreciate the real originality of a style. To do so, one should have read all the notable books in the order of their publication. It is at least possible to judge of the present, and also to accord some weight to the contemporary opinions of a work. Barbey d'Aurevilly found in Georges Sand a profusion of *anges de la destinée,* of *lampes de la foi,* and of *coupes de miel,* which certainly were not invented by her any more than the rest of her washed-out style; but "these decrepit tropes" would have been none the better if she had invented them. I feel sure that the cup, whose brim has been rubbed with honey, goes back to the obscure ages of pre-Hippocratic medicine. Hackneyed expressions enjoy a long life. M. Albalat notes justly "that there are images which can be renewed and rejuvenated." There are many such, and among them some of the commonest; but I cannot see that, in calling the moon the *morne lampe,* Leconte de Lisle has been very successful in freshening up Lamartine's *lampe d'or.* M. Albalat, who gives evidence of wide reading, should attempt a catalogue of metaphors by subject: the moon, the stars, the rose, the dawn, and all the "poetic" words. We should thus obtain a collection of a certain utility for the study of words and psychology of elementary emotions. Perhaps we should learn at last why the moon is so dear to poets. Meanwhile he announces his next book, *La Formation du style par l'assimilation des auteurs;* and I suppose that, once the series is complete, everyone will write well—that there will henceforth be a good medium style in literature, as there is in painting and in the other fine arts, which the State protects so successfully. Why not an Académie Albalat, as well as an Académie Julian?

Here, then, is a book which lacks almost nothing except not having a purpose, except being a work of pure and disinterested analysis; but, were it to have an influence, were it to multiply the number of honourable writers, it would deserve our maledictions. Instead of putting the manual of literature and all the arts within the reach of all, it would be wiser to transport their secrets to the top of some Himalaya. Yet there are no secrets. To be a writer, it is enough to have natural talent for the calling, to practise with perseverance, to learn a little more every morning, and to experience all human sensations. As for the art of "creating images," we are obliged to believe that this is absolutely independent of all literary culture, since the loveliest, truest and boldest images are enclosed in the words we use every day—age-old products of instinct, spontaneous flowering of the intellectual garden.

1899.

Subconscious Creation[1]

Certain men have received a special gift, which distinguishes them in a striking fashion from their fellows. The moment discus-throwers or generals, poets or clowns, sculptors or financiers rise above the common level, they demand the particular attention of the observer. The predominance of one of their faculties marks them out for analysis, and for that analytical method which consists in successive differentiation. We come thus to discern in mankind a class whose distinguishing trait is difference, just as, for common humanity, this trait is resemblance. There are men who let us know nothing of what they are going to say when they begin to speak. These are few. There are others who tell us all, as soon as they open their mouths. It is alleged that in this class there are marked disparities; for it is undeniable that, even among those who, at first sight, resemble each other most closely, there are no two creatures who are not, at bottom, contradictory. It is the highest glory of man, and the one that science has been unable to wrest from him, that there is no science of man.

If there be no science of the common man, still less is there a science of the different man, since the manifestation of this

---

[1] Suggested by *Physiologie cérébrale: Le Subconscient chez les artistes, les savants, et les écrivains,* by Dr. Paul Chabaneix, Paris, J.-B. Baillière. This study was already written when M. Ribot's masterly work, *L'Imagination créatrice* (July, 1900), appeared.

difference makes him solitary and unique, that is to say, incomparable. Yet, just as there is a general physiology, so there is a general psychology, also. Whatever their nature, all the beasts of the earth breathe the same air, and the brain of the genius, like that of the ordinary mortal, derives its primordial form from sensation. We have only a rough idea by what mechanism sensation is transformed into action. All we know is that the intervention of consciousness is not needed to bring about this transformation. We know also that this intervention may prove harmful through its power to modify the predetermined logic, to break the series of associations in order to create in the mind the first link of a new volitional chain.

Consciousness, which is the principle of liberty, is not the principle of art. It is possible to express quite clearly what has been conceived in the unconscious shades. Intellectual activity, far from being intimately allied with the functioning of consciousness, is more often disconcerted by it. We listen badly to a symphony, when we know we are listening. We think badly, when we know we are thinking. Consciousness of thinking is not thought.

The subconscious state is the state of automatic cerebration in full freedom, while intellectual activity pursues its course at the extreme limit of consciousness, a little below it and beyond its reach. Subconscious thought may remain for ever unknown. It may, on the other hand, come to light, either at the precise moment when the automatic activity ceases, or later—even after several years. These facts of cogitation do not, then, belong to the domain of the unconscious, properly speaking, since they can become conscious. Besides, it will doubtless be preferable to reserve to this rather vast word the meaning given it by a particular philosophy. The subconscious state differs also from the state of dreams, though dreams may be one of its manifestations. The dream is almost always absurd, with a special sort of absurdity, and is incoherent or orderly, according to its associations which are entirely passive,[2] and whose procession differs even from that of ordinary passive associations, conscious or unconscious.[3]

Imaginative intellectual creation is inseparable from the frequency of the subconscious state, and in this category of creations must be included the discovery of the scientist and the ideological construction of the philosopher. All who have invented or discovered something new in any field whatsoever, are imaginatives as well as observers. The most deliberate, the most thoughtful, the most painstaking writer is constantly, and in spite of himself, enriched by the effort of the subconscious. No work is so completely a product of the will that it does not

---

[2] See in a dream related by Maury *(Le Sommeil et les Rêves)* the word *jardin* causing the dreamer to visit Persia, then to read *L'Âne mort* (Jardin, Chardin, Janin); and in another dream, the syllable lo conducting the mind from the word *kilomètre* to *loto,* viâ *Gilolo, lobélia, Lopez.* However, the poet (by reason of rhyme or alliteration) experiences similar associations, but he must have the ability to render them logical, a thing which rarely happens in dreams pure and simple. Victor Hugo, a veritable incarnation of the Subconscious, rioted in these associations, which were at first involuntary.

[3] With regard to dreams, M. Chabaneix says (p. 17) that those who often think in visual images are subject to dreams in which the images are objectified in amplified form. A personal observation contradicts this, but in mentioning it I am only opposing a single observation to many observations. I refer to a writer who, although besieged, when awake, by internal visual images, sees images but rarely in dreams and never has any characteristic hallucinations. Recently, having reread Maury's book during the day, he experienced that night, for the first time, two or three vague hypnotic hallucinations, caused doubtless by the desire or fear of knowing this state…. This case may serve to explain the contagion of hallucination by books.—He saw kaleidoscopic flashes, then grinning heads, finally a figure clad in green, of life size, of whom the dreamer, looking out of the corner of his right eye, saw only one-half. At this moment, he was awaking. The figure evidently came from an illustrated history of Italian painting, which he had glanced at in the forenoon.

owe some beauty or novelty to the subconscious. No sentence, perhaps, however worked over, was ever spoken or written in absolute accord with the will. The search for the right word in the vast, deep reservoir of verbal memory is itself an act which escapes so completely from the control of the will, that very often the word on its way flees at the very moment when consciousness is about to perceive and to grasp it. Everyone knows how hard it is to find, by sheer force of will, the word wanted, and also with what ease and rapidity certain writers summon up, in the heat of composition, the rarest or the most appropriate words.

It is, however, imprudent to say: "Memory is always unconscious."[4] Memory is a secret pool where, unknown to us, the subconscious casts its net. But consciousness fishes there quite as readily. This pond, full of chance fish previously caught by sensation, is particularly well known to the subconscious. Consciousness is less skilful in provisioning itself from this source, though it has at its service several useful tricks, such as the logical association of ideas and the localization of images. Man acquires a different personality, according as the brain works in the darkness or by the lantern-light of consciousness; but, save in pathological cases, the second of these states is not so well defined that the first cannot intervene without interrupting the effort. It is under these conditions, and in accordance with this concert, that most works conceived, in the first instance either by the will or by the dream faculty, are completed.

In Newton's case (as a result of constant attention) the work of the subconscious is continuous, but connects itself periodically with voluntary activity. Now conscious, now unconscious, his thought explores all the possibilities. With Goethe, the sub-conscious is almost always active and ready to deliver to the will the multiple works which it elaborates without its aid

---

4 *Le Subconscient*, p. 11.

and far from it. Goethe himself has explained this in a marvellously lucid and instructive page:[5] "Every faculty of action, and consequently every talent, implies an instinctive force at work unconsciously and in ignorance of the rules whose principle is, however, implicit. The sooner a man becomes educated, the sooner he learns that there is a technique, an art, which will furnish him the means of attaining the regular development of his natural faculties. It would be impossible for what he acquires to injure in any way his original individuality. The supreme genius is he who assimilates and appropriates everything without prejudice to his innate character. Here we are confronted with the divers relations between consciousness and unconsciousness. Through an effort of exercise, of apprenticeship, of persistent and continuous reflection, through results obtained, whether good or bad, through the movements of resistance and attraction, the human organs amalgamate, combine unconsciously the instinctive and the acquired, and from this amalgam—from this chemistry at once conscious and unconscious—there issues at last a harmonious whole which fills the world with words. It is nearly sixty years since, in the full flush of my youth, the conception of *Faust* came to me perfectly clear and distinct, all its scenes unfolding before my eyes in the order of their succession. From that day the plan never left me, and living with it in view, I took it up in detail and composed, one after the other, those bits which, at the moment, interested me most, with the result that, when this interest has failed me, there have occurred gaps, as in the second part. The difficulty, at such points, was to obtain, by sheer force of will, what, in reality, is obtainable only by a spontaneous act of nature." It also happens conversely that a work conceived in advance and deferred in execution, comes at last to impose itself upon the will. The subconscious

---

5   Letter to W. von Humboldt, 17 March, 1832 *(Le Subconscient,* p. 16). Goethe was then eighty-three; he died five days later. The whole letter is quoted by Eckermann.

then seems to overflow and submerge the conscious, dictating things that are written only with repugnance. This is the obsession which nothing discourages, and which triumphs over even the most lackadaisical laziness, the most violent aversion. Later, once the work is completed, there is often experienced a sort of satisfaction. The idea of duty, which, ill understood, causes so many ravages in timid consciences, is no doubt an elaboration of the subconscious. Obsession is perhaps the force which impels to sacrifice, just as it is that which incites to suicide.

Schopenhauer used to compare the obscure and continuous effort of the unconscious, in the midst of impressions imprisoned in the memory, to rumination. This rumination, which is purely physiological, may suffice to modify convictions or beliefs. Hartmann discovered that a hostile idea, at first brushed aside, succeeded, after a certain time, in supplanting in his mind the idea which he was accustomed to entertain of man or of a fact: "If you wish or have the occasion to express your opinion upon the same subject, after days, weeks, or even months, you discover, to your great surprise, that you have undergone a veritable mental revolution—that you have completely abandoned opinions which, up to that time, you had firmly believed to be yours, and that new ideas have completely taken their place. I have often noted this unconscious processus of digestion and mental assimilation in my own case, and have always instinctively refrained from disturbing the process by premature reflection, whenever it involved important questions affecting my conceptions of the world and of the mind."[6] This observation might be extended to the exceedingly interesting problem of conversion. There is no doubt that people have suddenly felt themselves brought, or brought back, to religious ideas, when they had neither wish nor fear nor hope for this change. In conversion the will can act only after a long effort on the part of the

---

6 *Le Subconscient,* p. 24.

subconscious, and when all the elements of the new conviction have been secretly assembled and combined. This new force, which supports the convert, and whose origin is unknown to him, is what theology calls grace. Grace is the result of a subconscious effort. Grace is subconscious.

Like Hartmann, but instinctively, and not, in his case, by philosophic preconception, Alfred de Vigny entrusted to the subconscious the nurture of his ideas. When they were ripe, he recovered them. They came back of their own accord to offer themselves rich with all the consequences of their secret burgeoning. It may be supposed that, like Goethe, he was a subconscious whose promissory notes were on very long time, since Vigny left, between certain of his works, unusually long intervals. It is highly probable that, if there are individuals whose subconsciousness is inactive, there are others who, after a period of activity, cease suddenly to produce, either as a result of premature exhaustion, or through a modification in the relations of the brain cells. Racine offers the singular example of a twenty years' silence broken just halfway by two works which have only a formal resemblance to those of his first phase. Can it be supposed that it was through religious scruple that he so long refused to listen to the suggestions of the subconscious? Can it be supposed that religion, which had modified the nature of his perception, had, at the same time, diminished the physiological power of his brain? Such a supposition would run counter to all other observations, which go to show, on the contrary, that a new belief is a new excitant. It seems, then, probable that Racine became silent simply because he had almost nothing more to say. It is a common adventure, and he found in religion the common consolation.

A distinction should then be made between two sorts of subconscious individuals—those whose energy is short-lived and strong, and those whose force is less ardent but more sustained. The two extremes are exemplified by the man who produces a remarkable work in his early youth, then ceases, and by the man who offers for sixty years the spectacle of a mediocre, useless and continuous effort. I am speaking, of course, of those works in which the imaginative intelligence plays the major part—works in which the subconscious is always the master-collaborator.

More practically, and from a totally different point of view, M. Chabaneix, having studied the continuous subconscious, divides it into nocturnal and waking subconsciousness. If the former be a question of sleep or of the moments preceding sleep, it is oneiric or pre-oneiric. Maury, who was particularly afflicted by them, has carefully considered the hallucinations which are formed the moment the eyes close in sleep. It is not clear that these hallucinations which are called hypnagogic, and which are almost always visual, can have a special influence on the ideas undergoing elaboration in the brain. They are rather embryonic dreams which influence the course of the thought only as dreams influence it. It happens, at times, that the conscious effort of the brain is prolonged during the dream, even reaching its goal there, and that, on awaking, the dreamer finds himself, without reflection or difficulty, master of a problem, a poem, a combination, which had baffled him previously. Burdach, a Koenigsberg professor, made, in his dreams, several physiological discoveries which he was afterwards able to verify. A dream was sometimes the point of departure for an undertaking. Sometimes a work was entirely conceived and executed during sleep. It is highly probable, however, that it is the conscious reason which, at the moment of awaking, judges and rectifies the dream spontaneously, gives it its true value, and divests it of that incoherence peculiar to all dreams, even the most rational.

Inspiration, during the waking state, seems the clearest manifestation of the subconscious in the domain of intellectual creation. In its most pronounced form, it would seem to come very close to somnambulism. Certain attitudes of Socrates (according to Aulus Gellius), of Diderot, of Blake, of Shelley and of Balzac, give force to this opinion. Doctor Régis[7] says that almost all men of genius have been "waking sleepers" butt the waking sleeper is not infrequently an "absent-minded" individual—one whose mind tends to become concentrated upon a problem. Thus the excess and the absence of psychological consciousness would seem, in certain cases, to manifest themselves by identical phenomena. Of what did Socrates think days when he remained motionless? Did he think? Was he conscious of his thought? Do the fakirs think? And Beethoven, when, hatless and coatless, he let himself be arrested as a tramp? Was he under voluntary obsession, or in a quasi-somnambulistic condition? Did he know what he was pondering so deeply, or was his cerebral activity unconscious? John Stuart Mill composed his work on logic in the streets of London, as he went daily from his house to the offices of the India Company. Will anyone believe that this work was not planned in a state of perfect consciousness? What was subconscious in Mill, says M. Chabaneix, was the effort to make his way in a crowded street. "There was here automatism of the inferior centres." This reversal of terms—more frequent than certain psychologists have believed—may suggest doubts as to the true nature of inspiration. One ought at least to ascertain whether, from the moment when the realization—even purely cerebral—of a work begins, it is possible for this effort to remain wholly subconscious. Mozart's letter explains nobody but Mozart: "When I feel well and am in a good humour, whether riding in a carriage or taking a walk after a hearty meal, or at night when I cannot sleep, thoughts come thronging to me, and without the slightest effort. Where do they come from, and by what avenue do they reach me? I know nothing about it, have nothing to do with it. I keep in my

---

7 Preface to *Le Subconscient*.

head those that please me, and hum them—at least, so others have told me. Once I have my air, another soon comes to join it. The work grows, I hear it continually and get it more and more distinct, till at last the composition is entirely completed in my head, though it may be a long one.... All this takes place in me as in a beautiful, distinct dream.... If I start to write afterwards, I have nothing to do but to take out of the sack of my brain what has previously accumulated there, as I have explained to you. Thus it takes scarcely any time at all to put the whole thing on paper. Everything is already in perfect shape, and my score seldom differs very much from what I had in my head beforehand. It does not bother me to be interrupted while I am writing...."[8] With Mozart, the whole process is, therefore, subconscious, and the material labour of execution amounts to little more than mere copying.

I have seen a writer hesitate to correct his spontaneous composition for fear of marring the tone. He was aware that the state in which he corrected would be quite different from that in which he had written, and in which he had, at the same time, conceived his work. Often a word overheard, an attitude caught sight of, a singular individual passed in the street, gave him the sole suggestion for his tales, which he improvised in three or four hours. If he attempted to follow a preconceived plan, he almost always abandoned it after the first page, and finished his story in accordance with a new logic, reaching a conclusion quite different from that which had seemed best to him when he began. Some of these plans had been drafted under so strong a subconscious influence, that later he no longer understood them, recognized them only by the writing, and was able to determine their date only by the kind of paper he had used, and by the colour of the ink. On the contrary, other projects (for longer works) recurred to him quite

---

8   Jahm, quoted in *Le Subconscient,* p. 93.

frequently. He was conscious of thinking of them several times a day, and was convinced that it was these reveries, even when vague and inconsistent, that rendered the work of execution comparatively easy. In fact, I have never seen him seriously preoccupied with regard to works which were, however, supposed to be the result of a rather arduous effort. He never spoke of them, and I believe firmly that he never gave them a conscious thought till the moment when he wrote the terrible first lines. But, once the work was under way, almost all his intellectual life concentrated on it, the periods of subconscious rumination perpetually returning to join those of voluntary meditation.

As nearly as I have been able to make out, Villiers de l'Isle-Adam had this same method of working. Once an idea had entered his mind—and it sometimes entered quite suddenly, in the course of a conversation most often, for he was a great talker, and profited by everything—this idea, which had come in timidly and silently through the side-door, soon installed itself as if it were at home, and invaded all the reserve spaces of the subconscious. Then, from time to time, it rose to the conscious level, and really obliged Villiers to act under its obsession. At such moments, no matter who was with him, he talked. He talked even when he was alone. Indeed he always talked as if he were alone, when he talked of his idea. I heard thus, fragmentary, several of his last stories, and once when we were seated in front of a café on the boulevard, I had the impression that I was listening to veritable mental wanderings in which this assertion recurred periodically: "There was a cock! There was!" It was only some months later, when *Le Chant du Coq* appeared, that I understood. He spoke in a low voice, without addressing me. Yet his conscious aim, in thus turning over his ideas aloud, was to attempt to divine their effect upon a hearer. But, little by little, this purpose became obscured. It was the subconscious that was talking in his stead. He worked slowly. There exist five or six superimposed manuscripts of *L'Ève Future*, and the first differs so much from the last that Edison's name alone serves to link them together. It is often said of a man, who has written little, that he has done little work; but I am convinced that Villiers de l'Isle-Adam never stopped working an instant, even when asleep. In spite of the often absolute blockade that his ideas established about his attention, no mind ever worked more rapidly or was better gifted for conversation. He knew nothing of the twilight moments of awaking. After the fewest hours of sleep, he found himself, at a bound, in full possession of his verve and of his lucidity. Though, he was unquestionably the man of his books, it would, however, be possible to find in him the sketch of a dual personality, in which the conscious and unconscious so overlapped that it would be difficult to disentangle them. It would, on the other hand, be easy to write two lives of Mozart—one on the social individual, the other on the man in his second state, both perfectly legitimate.

Baudelaire used to say: "Inspiration means working every day"; but this aphorism does not appear to epitomize his personal experience. Regular daily work is, so to speak, inspiration regularized, domesticated, enslaved. These terms do not involve a contradiction, for it is certain that the second state can only gain in depth by becoming periodic. Habit, so powerful, reinforces nature to strengthen a psychological state which then comes to be a veritable necessity. Those who depart from a daily routine experience a certain uneasiness both during and after their regular working-hours—sometimes a real distress—especially if they remain in the same surroundings. Remorse has, perhaps, no other origin, whether it be connected with an habitual act which has not been accomplished, or with an act which is not habitual, and which has violently interrupted the customary procession of the days.

If inspiration be a second state, it may, then, be a second state induced voluntarily. There is no doubt that artists, writers, scientists can work without preparation when obliged to, spurred on only by necessity, and that, on the other hand, the work thus produced is quite as good as that done entirely for its own sake. This does not mean that the subconscious has remained inactive during the effort initiated by the will, but that its activity has been induced. There is, then, a subconscious state which is not spontaneous, which comes to mingle with the conscious when required by the will, but which, little by little, as the work progresses, substitutes itself for the will. It is often enough to set to work, in order to feel all the difficulties that had paralyzed effort vanish one by one; but perhaps this reasoning is paralogical, and the work has precisely become possible only because of the preliminary breaking-down of the obstacles which had confronted the mind in the first place. In either case, however, there is evident intervention of the subconscious forces.

How does a sensation become an image, the image an idea? How does the idea develop? How does it assume the form which seems best to us? How, in writing, is contribution levied upon the verbal memory? These are all questions which seem to me insoluble, yet whose solution would be necessary in order to formulate a precise definition of inspiration. "Neither reflection nor will-power can take the place of inspiration for the purpose of original creation," writes M. Ribot.[9] No doubt; but reflection and force of will may nevertheless have their rôle in the evolution of this mysterious phenomenon, and then, too; on the other hand, cases of pure intellectual automatism are rather rare. It must doubtless be supposed that those who are capable of experiencing the happy influence of inspiration, are also those most capable of feeling with force and with frequency the shocks of the external world. Imaginatives are also sensitives. Their brain reserves must be very rich in elements. This supposes a constant supply of sensations, as well as a very

---

9 *Psychologie des Sentiments.*—W. von Humboldt said: "Reason combines, modifies and directs; it cannot create, because the vital principle is not in it" *(Ideas on the New French Constitution)*.

lively sensibility and an incessantly renewed capacity for feeling. This sensibility, too, belongs, in large part, to the domain of the subconscious. There are, according to Leibnitz's expression, "thoughts which our soul does not perceive." There are also sensations which our senses do not perceive, and it is perhaps these sensations which leave our brain as they entered it—subconsciously. The most fruitful observations are those which we make without knowing it. To live without thinking of life is often the best means for coming to know life. After half a century and more, a man sees the surroundings, the scenes, and the events of his unreflecting childhood rise before him. As a child, he had dwelt in the external world as in an extension of himself, with a purely physiological concern. He had seen without seeing. Yet now, while the middle distance remains veiled in mist, it is this period of his most fleeting impressions that returns and takes on life before his eyes. It is very evident that the sensation, which has entered us without our being aware of it, can never, at any moment, be voluntarily evoked; but the conscious sensation, on the contrary, can return suddenly, without any assistance from the will. The subconscious has, then, dominion over two orders of sensations, whereas consciousness has but one at its disposal. This may explain why will and reflection have so restricted a share in the creations of literature and of art.

But what is their rôle in the rest of life?

In principle, man is an automaton, and it would seem that in him consciousness is an acquisition, an added faculty. Let us not be deceived. Because man walks, acts, talks, he is not necessarily conscious, nor is he ever completely conscious. Consciousness, if we take the word in its precise, absolute sense, is without doubt the possession of the few. In crowds men become particularly automatic. Indeed, their very instinct to herd together, to do all of them the same thing at the same time, is unmistakable evidence as to the nature of their intelligence. How can we suppose consciousness and will to exist in the members of those dense throngs which, on days of festivals or during disorders, move forward in a mass toward the same point, with the same cries and the same gestures? They are ants, that come out from under the blades of grass after a rain, and nothing more. The conscious man, who mingles without reflection in the crowd, who acts as the crowd acts, loses his personality. He is now merely one of the tentacles of the great artificial octopus, and almost all his sensations die away in the collective brain of the hypothetical animal. From this contact he will bring back next to nothing. The man who comes out of the crowd, like the man saved from drowning, has one recollection only—that of having fallen into the water.

It is among the small number of the conscious élite that must be sought the veritably superior examples of a humanity of which they are, not the leaders—that would be a pity, and too contrary to instinct—but the judges. However—and this is a subject for serious meditation—these individuals, raised above the rest, attain their full power only at moments when the conscious, becoming subconscious, opens the locks of the brain and lets the renewed floods of sensation rush back to the world whence they were derived. They are magnificent instruments on which the subconscious alone plays with genius, for it, too, is subconscious. Goethe is the type of these dual men, and the supreme hero of intellectual humanity.

There are other men, not less rare, but less complete, in whom the will plays but a very ordinary rôle, and who are nothing the moment they cease to be under the influence of the subconscious. Their genius is often only the purer and more energetic because of this. They are more docile instruments under the breath of the unknown God. But, like Mozart, they do not know what they do. They obey an irresistible force. That is why Gluck had his piano moved out into the middle of a meadow, in the full sunlight. That is why Haydn gazed at a ring, why Crébillon lived surrounded by dogs, why Schiller frequently inhaled the odour of rotten apples with which he had filled the drawer of his table. Such are the most innocent fantasies of the subconscious. There are others that are both more insistent and more terrible.

The Roots of Idealism

I

Since writing, in *Physique de l'Amour*, the chapter on "The Tyranny of the Nervous System," with its criticism of Lamarck's saying, "the environment creates the organ," I have come to conceive some doubts on the legitimacy of my ideas. I am going to state them without definitely taking sides either against myself or against subjective idealism, to which in the last analysis I remain in large part faithful.

Idealism is today the dominant doctrine in philosophy, which was bound to come to it, after a period of raillery, for reasoning leads to it invincibly.

We know that there are two idealisms. It is then prudent, whenever this word is employed in a context not purely philosophic, to define it. There are two idealisms, both qualified by a word which is identical in form, but different in meaning, since one comes from *ideal,* the other from *idea*. The former is the expression of a moral or religious state of mind. It is very nearly synonymous with spiritualism, and it is this that M. Brunetière employs when that hard-hearted man becomes sentimental on the subject of the "renaissance of idealism." There is a certain "Revue Idéaliste," marked by a serene religious sentiment, which belongs to the same clan, and in which it would be a mistake to seek any enlightenment on Berkeley's doctrine.

The other idealism, which it would have been better to call ideaism, and which Nietzsche has carried to the point of phenomenalism, is a philosophical conception of the world. Schopenhauer, who was not its inventor, has provided it with its best formula—the world is my representation. That is to say, the world is such as it appears to me. If it has a real existence in itself, it is inaccessible to me. It is that which I see it, or feel it, to be.

Schopenhauer's formula withstands every criticism. It is irrefutable. The doctrine which derives from it, if attacked directly, presents itself as an impregnable fortress. Every reasoning blunts itself impotently against it. It has this remarkable quality, that it is as valid for the sensation, for the sentiment, as for the idea. There may be based upon it equally, at will, a theory of intelligence, like Taine's, or a theory of sensibility—something which has not been yet attempted. Take the hackneyed statement that the same painful event does not affect with the same intensity two persons whom it strikes with the same external force. That is idealism. Take the subject of tastes and of colours (in which Nietzsche found so much amusement). There too, we have idealism. Whenever we study life, facts, intelligences, physiologies, sensibilities for the purpose of finding, not resemblances, but differences, we are practising idealism. While there is life, there is idealism. That is to say, there are, according to the species, or even the individual, different ways of reacting against an external or internal sensation. Everything is merely representation, for a bird as well as for a man, for a crab as for a cuttle-fish. Reality is relative. A woman, a nervous man even, can suffer intensely—perhaps lose consciousness—by imagining the amputation of a leg, the scraping of the bones. Hardened soldiers, on the contrary, have undergone such operations without flinching. A particular taste for cruelty should not be attributed to the civilizations which countenanced torture, and to those which still practise it. The refinements which the Chinese bring to physical punishment are nothing but a very clear indication of insensibility. That which agonizes a European makes a yellow man smile. But there are, among men of the same social group, numerous degrees of sensibility. Pain, like pleasure, is a representation. The formula has been extended to groups. A people is what it believes itself to be, very much more than what it actually is. Most social disorders are merely collective representations.

But it is difficult to explain idealism by an examination of the facts of sensibility. They are too well known, too generally admitted, to support a philosophic construction. A point of departure more extraordinary and less easy to understand is needed. The phenomenon of vision is generally employed in this connection. It seems simple, but, when analyzed, it is exceedingly mysterious.

Seeing is the most natural thing in the world. Yet, what do we see, when we see a tree? A tree, to be sure, but not the tree itself. What enters us, as object perceived, is not the tree as tree, but the tree as image. What is the image worth? Is it exact?

So it may be supposed, since it is sensibly the same for the various persons who perceive it, and since divergences of appreciation begin only when there come into play judgments conditioned by sentiment or interest. This supposed exactitude is, in any case, very relative. An image is an image, a photograph, and it differs from the reality-tree (pure hypothesis) as much as a round, long, branching, leafy object differs from a graphic representation, without thickness. It is true that tactile sensation, or its memory, comes then to our aid, adding to the tenuousness of the visual image the idea of consistence, of resistance, without which we have difficulty in conceiving matter. We can then—and thanks also to our observation of the opposing play of light and shade—give this vain image its true position in space.

But however complete and concordant may be the actions of our senses, when it is a question of knowing an object—even when, as in sexual love, the six senses, including the genital sense, come into play simultaneously—it is none the less the fact that the object known remains exterior to ourselves. Besides, this qualification "known" is little appropriate to the object perceived, since it has an interior face, inaccessible at first glance to our senses. If we are dealing with a living being—and all the more if this being be intelligent and complex—we must exercise all sorts of faculties and devote ourselves to minute analyses in order to arrive, even then, at a knowledge that is very nearly illusory.

Knowledge arrives, then, at a certain bankruptcy. It is not very far from this point to that of proclaiming the uselessness of the external world as a means of explaining the nature of knowledge itself. It is only a step from uselessness to reality. The idealistic philosophers who develop their theory to its logical conclusion, can say, without paradox, that everything occurs in vision, for example, as if the object did not exist—as if intelligence, though believing that it receives aid from the eye, in reality created this object just as far as it wishes to know it. The phenomenon of hallucinations gives an appearance of reason to these exasperated idealists. Did not Taine, who was not exasperated, call sensation a true hallucination? But why true? That is a word which, in the circumstances, it is difficult to justify. It would be juster to say that hereditary habit inclines us to regard certain sensations as true, certain others as false. Perhaps utility serves us also as guide, and we imagine, in order to reassure ourselves, an external and fallacious world whose operations correspond to the movements of our psychology.

II

There is another way of knowing, at once more elementary, more intimate, and more uncertain. This is absorption. The elements of our nourishment, in proportion as we "know" them, disintegrate, yield soluble parts to our organism, and reject the rest in a form equally unknowable. If we reject, as we should, the primitive distinction between soul and body, admitting only the body and believing everything to be physical, then this way of knowing should be studied parallel with those ways which spring from each of our different senses, or from their collaboration. It is certain that absorption has taught man in every age. It is through it, and not by virtue of an unknown instinct, that he has succeeded in separating vegetables and animals into good and bad, into useful and harmful or indifferent. Our analytical methods are still unable, save perhaps in particularly expert hands, to distinguish mushrooms as a harmful or favourable form of nourishment. The expert himself must be guided, for this delicate operation, by a direct and real experiment of absorption. Man, devoid of science, took himself as laboratory. None was surer. He acquired, by this means, certain parts of his knowledge which have proved most useful to humanity and to the domestic animals. From time to time medications are rediscovered which figure in ancient pharmacopeias. Thus formate of lime or of soda, recently prescribed as a muscular invigorant, contains scarcely a principle that did not figure in the old "water of magnanimity," obtained by maceration and distillation of a certain quantity of ants. How did our ancestors, who were no doubt shepherds and labourers, come to distinguish the virtue of ants? Evidently by eating them. The foul Arabs and other low forms of humanity who eat their vermin, find in them, perhaps, an analogous tonic. This practice, like all those which resolve themselves into absorption, is assuredly dictated by experience. Neither a man nor an animal can, in principle, become addicted to an act which is harmful to him. Between acts that are harmful, and acts that are salutary, there is a whole series of games, but it is difficult to admit that a daily game is a harmful act.

Why do not peasants eat certain abundant rodents? It is easy to answer by offering taste and disgust as pretexts; but this is reversing the logical order of the terms of the argument.

A food does not disgust by its odour. The odour of a food disgusts because this food is harmful or useless. To understand this, without the necessity of insisting upon it, it is enough to think of all those foods with nauseous odours, which we appreciate much more than those which might be considered pleasant. Such is the fruit of experience, that is to say, of knowledge.

I believe that absorption should be considered one of the best means we have of appreciating the practical value of certain parts of the external world. Agriculture, kitchen-gardening, cooking, pharmacy almost entirely, are born of it. Assuredly men, even the rarest chemists and physiologists, could suck a kola-nut for years, without suspecting those virtues that savages found quite simply by cracking it with their teeth.

They jest who, ignoring not only the importance but the very existence of this sixth or seventh or tenth sense, attribute to taste or to smell a mysterious power of divining the harmfulness of a plant or of its fruit. How can they help seeing immediately that this preservative instinct, if it be hereditary, has had a beginning, and that, at this beginning, there was a fact of knowledge? The traditional notion of instinct must be left in the old theological and spiritualistic repertories. It serves simple people as an easy means of distinguishing man from the animals. Animals have instinct, man has intelligence. There are proofs. Man poisons himself with mushrooms, frugivorous animals never. What man? Not the traditional peasant surely.

Only the *déraciné* or the city-dweller, who has naturally lost an instinct which was useless to him. This proof proves only that it is dangerous for man, as for the other animals, or for plaints themselves, to change their habitat. There is a painful, uncertain transitory phase. It is during this phase that we go into the woods, picknicking, and gather toadstools. But rabbits in cages, when given wet grass or vegetables instinctively unknown to them, allow themselves to be completely poisoned. Free, it would never have occurred to them to crop at dewfall, because their ancestors, dwelling in extremely thick woodlands, were ignorant of the very existence of the dew, and transmitted distrust of wet grass to their offspring.

Man, even in the state of semi-civilization, is burdened with too much knowledge for it all to be transmitted hereditarily; but there is no doubt that the oldest and most useful reaches us in this manner. When we walk in the forest there are berries that tempt us, whortleberries, for example, but never alderberries. Who has taught us (I am supposing a real ignorance), that they are purgative and even dangerous? Instinct? What is instinct? The hereditary transmission of knowledge.

This transmission can, without doubt, occur in the case of abstract ideas, as well as of practical ideas—that is to say, useful for the conservation of life. Some, besides, are really useful, and even primordial. It is as reasonable to believe that they are inherited as to suppose them personally acquired. It might be possible to rehabilitate the theory of innate ideas, by revising it carefully and eliminating from its catalogue all sorts of Platonic or Christian inventions, too recent to have entered our blood.

As to the direct knowledge of ideas, this is gained in a form sensibly analogous to the knowledge of matter by absorption. Once they have entered us, ideas either remain inert, unknown, or else are disintegrated. In the first case, it is not long before they are expelled from the brain, much like an indigestible morsel which has entered the intestines. Their stay may produce a certain irritation, even lesions. That is to say, it may provoke absurd acts, manifestly without logical relation to the normal physiology of the patient. This effect may be observed in all countries, but especially in France, at the time of great political or moral crises. We see people tormented by the presence of a parasitic idea in their brain, like sheep by the residence of a trumpet-fly's egg in their frontal sinus. Man, like the sheep, has the "itch." That ends badly for the sheep—for the man also, very often.

In the second case, the external ideas that have entered the brain are disintegrated there and unite their atoms with the other atomic knowledge already within us. An idea is digested, assimilated. Assimilated, it then becomes very different from what it was when it entered the intelligence. Like intestinal absorption, mental absorption is, therefore, an excellent though indirect way of acquiring knowledge. In both cases, the ideas, like the aliments, will be known, not immediately, but by their effects. Thus men know hereditarily that certain ideas are individual or social poisons, and that others are equally favourable to the welfare of the individual or to the development of a people. But, in this order, notions of utility and of harmfulness are much less precise. We have seen a certain idea, reputed to be very dangerous, contributing to the health of a man, of a family, of a society, of civilization itself. Ideas are extremely workable, plastic. They take the shape of the brain. There are perhaps no ideas that are bad for a healthy brain whose form is normal. There are perhaps no good ones for a brain that is sick and warped.

III

But let us come back to our tree or our ox. This ox can enter us in one of two ways. First, partly, but really, in the form of food. What we absorb of it in that way cannot, evidently, be known as ox. It reaches our knowledge only through its effects—strength, health, gaiety, activity, depression. Even were this absorption total in the case of a small animal, digestible in all its parts, the result, from the point of view of immediate knowledge, would be the same, since the object becomes resolved into elements which render its form unknowable.

The other manner—that which brings into play the external senses—will make us know the ox, in appearance as such, in reality as image of an ox. What is the true value of this knowledge? We must here return to this question, in order to enter more easily upon the second part of this essay.

Truth has been very seriously defined as conformity of the representation of an object with this object itself. But that solves nothing. What is the object itself, since we can know it only as representation? It is useless to carry the discussion further. We shall turn indefinitely around the fortress of idealism, without ever finding an opening, or any weak point. We shall enter it never, no argument serving as a bomb against its solid walls.

However, we must consider carefully. Having thoroughly reflected, we shall ask if this fortress be real, or if, on the contrary, it be not, perhaps, a representation without object, a pure phantom, like those sunken cities whose bells still ring for great festivals, but are heard only by those who believe in their mysterious life. This doubt will lead us to re-examine the reasoning of Berkeley and of Kant, and see if it be well constructed. Does it start from the senses to reach the mind? Or may it not, perchance, be one of those mental conceptions which fall back upon the senses like an avalanche, freezing and smothering them?

How have the senses been formed? Such is the question. Has there always been an opposition between the ego and the non-ego? There is nothing in the intelligence that has not first been in the senses. By intelligence, we must in this philosophic dictum, due to Locke, understand the psychologic consciousness. Let us leave aside the consciousness, which can only serve to complicate the problem. Consciousness is a phenomenon of secondary order and of an entirely sentimental utility, if it be restricted to man; commonplace and of pure reflex, if extended to all sensible matter. Let us consider this matter in perhaps its humblest manifestations, taking account only of the actions and reactions, exactly as we might observe the influence of heat, of light, or of cold on milk, wine or water. In living matter there will, however, be something more—the decomposition will be compensated by assimilation, and if the assimilation be abundant, there will be generation. Other forms, resembling the first, will detach themselves from the matrix form. This represents life essentially, a living being, a being limited in duration by the very fact of its growth, which constitutes an effort and a loss. Let us consider a being whose senses are not differentiated, and let us see how it gets on with the rest of the world, how it knows it.

The amoeba has no exterior senses. It is an almost homogeneous mass, and yet it is sensible to almost the same sensorial impressions as the highest mammal. It feeds (smell and taste); it moves (sense of space, touch); it is sensible to light, at least to certain rays (sight); its environment being in perpetual movement, ceaselessly traversed by sonorous waves, it doubtless reacts to these vibrations (hearing). Perhaps, even, it possesses, without special organs, senses which we lack, and which we recover only by study and analysis, such as the chemical sense, which judges the composition of a body, declares it assimilable or counsels its rejection. The exercise of all these senses denotes, first of all, a very long heredity. They have, doubtless, been acquired successively only, unless, the absence of one of them being capable of causing death, their presence is the strict consequence of the life of this humble beast. But it is useless to construct any hypotheses on the subject. It is enough to keep to the fact, and this fact is the existence of a being without differentiated organs, that is to say, a being all of whose parts are equally adapted to react against every external excitation.

Why these reactions? They are one of the conditions of life. But could not life be conceived without them? It is possible. It is a question of environment. If the amoeba's environment were homogeneous and calm, if it were of a constant temperature and luminosity, if it furnished an abundance of proper nourishment, if, in a word, the animal dwelt in an alimentary bath, no reactions would be necessary, and its only movement would be to open its pores for food, to reject the excess of this food, to divide itself, when swollen, into two amoebas. Why, then, does it possess all these senses which, though unorganized, are perfectly real? Because the environment obliges it to have them, because of its instability. The senses, whether differentiated, or spread over the entire surface of a living form, are the creation of the environment which—light, sound, material exteriority, odours, etc.—acts in accordance with different discontinuous manifestations. Constant or continuous, they would be without effect. Discontinuous, they make themselves felt. Discontinuous light has created the eye, just as the drop of water creates a hole in granite.

A being, whatever it may be, whether vague and almost amorphous or clearly defined, is not isolated in the universal vital environment. It is the molecule of a diapason. It vibrates, not of its own accord, but in obedience to a general movement. The living cell, itself in internal movement and subjected to all the reactions of external movement, perceives this movement doubtless as an unique impression only. But when several cells come together and live in permanent contact, the impressions of external movement begin to be perceived as differentiated. Is this then necessary? Do there then already exist luminous vibrations, different from sonorous vibrations? Assuredly, since otherwise the sensorial differentiation would be inexplicable, being useless. The union of several cells permits the animal to divide its work of perception, and to present to each perceptible manifestation an organ or, at least, the sketch of an organ, appropriate to receive it.

It would be possible, it is true, from the idealistic point of view, to suppose that the senses are a creation of the individual, an enhancement of his own life, and that he differentiates, on his own initiative, his cinematic impression. This would be a phenomenon of spontaneous analytic creation, the analyzing instrument existing prior to the matter analyzed, or even, for exasperated idealists, creating this matter according to determinate needs, once and for all, by its own physiology. It would then be a property of organized living matter to fabricate senses for itself, and to diversify, by this means, its own life. This point of view is not easy to admit for several reasons, purely physical.

First, if this sensorial differentiation were a faculty of living matter, it would not be observed to be limited in its powers, as it is. Even admitting certain senses unknown to man, such as the chemical sense, the electric sense, the sense of orientation (extremely doubtful), it is still seen that the number of senses is very limited. But, far more important, the fundamental senses are found to be identical among the majority of the higher species, vertebrates and insects, with very few exceptions. The moment the animal arrives at sensorial differentiation, this differentiation occurs in response to the manifestations of matter.

The senses should, then, correspond to external realities. They have been created, not by the perceiving being, but by the perceptible environment. It is the light that has created the eye, just as, in our houses, it has created the windows. Where there is no light, fish become blind. This is perhaps the direct proof, for if light is the creation of the eye, this creation can occur at the bottom of the sea quite as well as on the surface of the earth. Another proof: these same fish, having become blind, but still requiring a luminous habitat, create for themselves in the night of the abysses, not eyes, but apparatus directly productive of light; and this artificial light creates anew the atrophied eye. The senses are then clearly the product of the environment. That is all they can do, moreover, their utility being nil, if the environment is not perceptible. It might still be objected that it is the nervous system which, having intuition of an environment to be perceived, creates for itself organs adapted to this perception. But this is merely begging the question; for, either the nervous system has knowledge of the external environment, which means that it already has senses, or else it has no senses, and thus can have no knowledge. A more serious objection would be that, sensorial aptitude being a property of the nervous system, it would afterwards create for itself organs in order to perceive more distinctly, and clearly differentiated, the various natural phenomena. This view would explain up to a certain point the creation of sensorial organs, but not the existence of the senses themselves as sensitive power. It is, moreover, certain that the nervous system acts rather by tyrannizing the organs at its disposal, than by seeking to modify these organs or to create new ones. It is a power which evidently exceeds the limits of its capacity. It has, on the contrary, devolved upon the external phenomena which, in acting mechanically on the living matter, produce in it local modifications. The organs of the senses seem to be nothing other than surfaces sensitized by the very agents which, once their work is done, will reflect in them their particular physiognomy. The eye—let us take once more this example, and repeat it—is a creation of light.

Since they are themselves the work of the principal general phenomena, the senses ought then to agree exactly—allowing for approximation—with the very nature which has created them. The luminous environment is not, in this case, a dream, but a reality, and a reality existing prior to the eye which perceives it; and, since the eye is the very product of light, objects situated in this luminous environment should be perceived by it as an exact image, just as the drill which creates a hole, creates it strictly to its size, its form, its image. Bacon said that the senses are holes. Here this is only a metaphor.

IV

There remains the question of the co-ordination of the impressions received materially by the senses. This co-ordination, for elementary sensations, is evidently identical for all beings. The snail, his horn being threatened, and man, his eye, make the same shrinking movement. Identical acts can have as cause only identical realities, or ones perceived as such. With judgment, we enter upon the mystery. If light is constant, the judgment which admits its existence is variable according to the species, and, in the higher species, according to the individual. It is clear that all eyes are affected by light, but we do not know to what degree, or according to what mode of spectral decomposition. It is the same for all other senses. Even if the reality of the sensible world be admitted, we are obliged to pronounce cautiously upon the quality of this reality, as reality perceived and judged. We then return to idealism, though having had a quite different end in view. We must retrace our steps, contemplate anew the ironic portress, and resign ourselves never to know anything save appearance.

Another fact, however, remains—another fortress, perhaps, reared facing the other. This is, that matter existed before life. The gain seems slight, but it is equivalent to saying that the phenomena perceived by the senses are exterior to the senses which now perceive them; and this perhaps means that, if life becomes extinct, matter will survive life. The proposition of the idealists that the world would come to an end if there were no longer any sensibilities capable of feeling it, any intelligences capable of perceiving it, seems, therefore, untenable. And yet what would a world be, that was neither thought nor felt? We must recognize this, that when we think of a world void of thought, it still contains our thought, or it is our thought which contains it and animates it. Another phenomenon analogous to this has, perhaps, contributed much to belief in the immortality of the soul, namely, that we cannot conceive of ourselves as dead save by thinking of this death, by feeling and seeing it. The idea of our non-existence supposes, moreover, the life of our thought. That there is here an illusion due to the very functioning of the mechanism of thought is probable enough; but it is difficult not to take it into account. It would seem somewhat high-handed to make abstraction of it.

We can attempt it, however, and try a new road leading "beyond thought." The way would be to consider the general movement of the things in which our thought itself is closely implicated, and by which it is rigorously conditioned. Far, perhaps, from thought thinking life, it is life that animates thought. What is anterior is a vast rhythmic undulation, of which thought is but one of the moments, one of the bounds.

The position taken by man outside the world to judge the world, is a factitious attitude. It is, perhaps, only a game, and one that is too easy. The division of man into two parts, thought, physical being, one considering the other and pretending to contain it, is only a philosophic amusement which becomes impossible the moment we stop to consider. There is, in fact, a physic of thought. We know that it is a product, measurable, ponderable. Unformulated externally, it nevertheless manifests its physical existence by the weight which it imposes upon the nervous system. It needs speech, writing, or some sort of sign, in order to manifest itself externally. Telepathy, thought, penetration, presentiment—if there be any facts in this category which have really been verified—would in such a case be so many proofs of the materiality of thought. But it is useless to multiply arguments in favour of a fact which is no longer contested save by theology.

This fact of materiality gives thought a secondary place. It is produced. It might not be. It is not primordial. It is a result, a consequence—doubtless a property of the nervous system, or even of living matter. It is then through a singular abuse, that we have become accustomed to consider it isolated from the ensemble of its producing causes.

But, if thought be a product, it is, none the less, productive in its turn. It does not create the world, it judges it. It does not destroy it, it modifies and reduces it to its measure. To know is to frame a judgment; but every judgment is arbitrary, since it is an accommodation, an average, and since two different physiologies give different averages, just as they give different extremes. The path, once again, after many windings, brings us back to idealism.

Idealism is definitely founded on the very materiality of thought, considered as a physiological product. The conception of an external world exactly knowable is compatible only with belief in the reason, that is to say, in the soul, that is to say, furthermore, in the existence of an unchangeable, incorruptible, immortal principle, whose judgments are infallible. If, on the contrary, knowledge of the world be the work of a humble physiological product, thought—a product differing in quality, in modality, from man to man, species to species—the world may perhaps be considered as unknowable, since each brain or each nervous system derived from its vision and from its contact a different image, or one which, if it was at first the same for all, is profoundly modified in its final representation by the intervention of the individual judgment.

If the same object produces the same image on the retina of an ox or the retina of a man, it will not, doubtless, be concluded, therefore, that this image is known and judged identically by the ox and the man.

There are no two leaves, there are no two beings, alike in nature. Such is the basis of idealism and the cause of incompatibility with the agreeable doctrines with which men continue to be entertained.

The reasons of idealism plunge deep down into matter. Idealism means materialism, and conversely, materialism means idealism.

1904.

ALSO AVAILABLE FROM ANTIPODES PRESS

Very Woman
BY REMY DE GOURMONT

Hubert Entragues, aesthete and litterateur, conceives a passion for the ethereal Sixtine in this "cerebral novel" of 1890. The romance remains largely imaginary, a pursuit localized in the skull of the intellectual Entragues. Alone with his thoughts and his literature, his baroque reflections careen from lyrical exaltation to sullen despondency according to the inscrutable actions of his elusive inamorata. In his refined loneliness, his lucid and sensual daydreams develop into a story within the story, mirroring and embellishing the inner experience of their author.

Very Woman is a masterpiece of the symbolist movement of fin de siècle literature. A brilliant stylist, Gourmont's luxurious, poetic prose is full of erudition, irony, and eroticism, creating an atmosphere all its own.

Paperback: 226 pages. ISBN: 978-0-9882026-8-9.

www.ingramcontent.com/pod-product-compliance
Lightning Source LLC
Chambersburg PA
CBHW022228010526
44113CB00033B/648